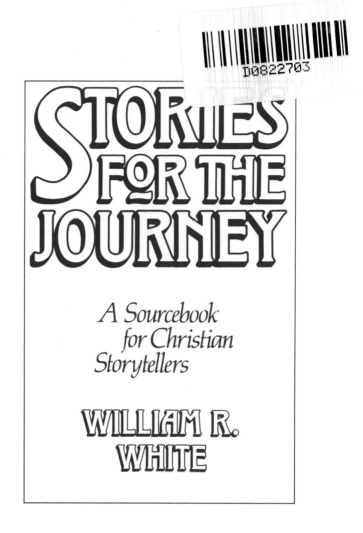

STORIES FOR THE JOURNEY

A Sourcebook for Christian Storytellers

WILLIAM R. WHITE

AUGSBURG Publishing House • Minneapolis

To Norm, my first story partner

STORIES FOR THE JOURNEY
A Sourcebook for Christian Storytellers

ISBN 0-8066-2364-0   LCCN 88-47910

Manufactured in the U.S.A.   APH 10-6026

            9   0   1   2   3   4   5   6   7   8   9

CONTENTS

PREFACE

From the earliest days of Christianity followers of Jesus have used "the journey" as a metaphor for the Christian life. The Acts of the Apostles tells us that the first Christians called themselves The Way. John Bunyan's classic, *Pilgrim's Progress,* perhaps, is the most famous treatment of this idea.

The stories I have included for your faith journey have been collected during my own. Many of these tales were discovered in books (see the bibliography) while others were found in conversations. Over dinner in the Wartburg Seminary cafeteria, students from Ethiopia who had listened to some of my stories told me tales from their native land. In a late night bull session following my presentation at the Institute for Christian Living in Midland, Texas, I was again the listener. Still other stories arrived by mail, from friends and readers of my previous collections, *Speaking in Stories* and *Stories for Telling.*

A number of the stories arrived without a listed source. With a little help from my friends and a lot of help from the reference librarians at Central Michigan University, I have traced down most of the stories that are included. In a few cases the search was unsuccessful.

I am grateful to Tom Boomershine, Gigi Conners, Shelia Dailey, Bill Eisenmann, Betty Lou Grace, William Gary Kobs, Tennagie Negussie, Ralph Smith, and George Zorn for their help in finding stories.

George and Marilyn Zorn read the manuscript carefully and offered many helpful suggestions. Sally White has read every draft and listened patiently to many oral presentations. Shelia Dailey not only has provided me the ear of another storyteller, but allowed me to use her fine study of C. S. Lewis in the opening chapter. I am most grateful.

I am not a folklorist. I am a pastor who reads and collects stories, all kinds of stories. I collect with an eye for those tales that I find most helpful in my preaching, teaching, and counseling. Where possible I retain the original version of a story. When necessary I change or adapt a story in order that it might be used with and for the people I serve. I assume the reader will do the same.

1

WITH ALL YOUR MIND

Hear, O Israel, the Lord our God, the Lord is one. Love the Lord your God with all your heart and with all your soul and with all your mind.   Mark 12:29-30

Creation, like our God, is one. Everything is connected to everything else.

> All things by immortal power
> hiddenly
> together linked are
> Thou cannot disturb a flower
> without troubling a star.[1]

Human beings, both corporately and individually, are one. The Hebrew people rejected a Greek dualism that separated the body from the soul. We do not have a body; we are a body. We do not have a soul; we are a soul.

Since everything finds its center in creation's single unifying presence, everything sings of the glory of God. In this spirit the psalmist urges that all instruments be tuned for praise. All of life is lived in thanksgiving to our gracious God.

Our acts of praise are responses to God who uses every means possible to communicate with us. Scripture reports that God spoke through dreams and visions as well as exhortations. Scripture is a many-splendored thing mixing parable, narrative, poetry, hymn, proverb, and fable with arguments and concepts. All the tools of human communication were used by God to address the people and in turn God's people spoke with many voices to extol the wonders of the one God.

In the contemporary church we appear to have a much narrower arsenal for proclamation. Most serious oral and written communication about God is limited to ideas and concepts. Seldom do we find stories, hymns, or poetry in the body of a major theological presentation, other than by way of brief illustration.

It is not that modern forces take issue with the Hebrew wholistic understanding of life. Science continues to make "discoveries" that support the unity of existence. Biology and psychiatry reject a separation of soul and body. Medicine uses the term *psychosomatic* to affirm that our emotions are not separate from our bodies. Either can cause illness. Both are necessary for health.

Human life is such a unity that hearing and believing, faith and action, religion and ethics cannot be separated. Human beings do not have a religious section or part. The command to love God with our whole heart, soul, and mind reminds us that our whole being was made for God.

The two hemisphere theory

One of science's discoveries of wholism is the "two brain" or "two hemisphere" theory. This theory says that the left and right hemispheres of the brain have quite different functions. According to theorists, the left hemisphere is the center for speech, logic, and analysis. It deals with math, grammar, and abstract thinking.

The right hemisphere handles spatial relations and perceives shapes, sizes, textures, and colors. It is the part of the brain where dreams, imagination, and feelings originate.

Though it has two hemispheres, there is but one brain. The functions may be different, but learning takes place through both. The two hemisphere theory encourages those who teach to address the whole mind, both its rational and imaginative aspects. Like our theology, our teaching should be wholistic.

Not everyone who uses the two hemisphere theory focuses on unity. By labeling people as "left brainers" or "right brainers"—as if it is possible to only use one hemisphere—some writers seem bent on dividing human life. Others seem to pit one hemisphere against another by arguing the merits of the left or the right brain over the other.

Our interest is to encourage Christian teachers and preachers to use the whole brain, since it is clear that human beings need both hemispheres to be fully human. Only if teaching is wholistic will we help people love God with their whole minds.

Unfortunately, most of our teaching and education is directed to the left hemisphere, the rational part of the brain that our culture tends to overvalue. "Real" adult learning leans on information and facts. Most "serious" theology ignores imagination or feeling. Many people are deeply suspicious of emotions and even in music there is a tendency among mainline Christian groups to focus on the more cerebral hymns, leaving songs of emotion to the conservative churches.

New Testament scholar Walter Wink uses the two hemisphere theory in his fine book, *Transforming Bible Study.* In it he concludes he can no longer do biblical exegesis in the traditional way. It "simply does not use enough of the brain, the person, the self," Wink writes. "We must get our whole selves involved with it, right brain as well, and struggle to let it endow us with a fuller share of our available humanity."[2]

Wink is concerned that we understand the Scriptures are not

directed only to the left hemisphere. The biblical text is full of metaphors, parables, poems, and other gems that are offered through and for the right brain. If we are to love God with our whole mind we cannot ignore information and facts, but neither can we expend all our energy on verbal discourse.

The issue is more than a matter of taste, more than a question of whether one prefers a more rational or imaginative presentation of religion. Just how do we come to faith? The church's traditional answer has been that faith is a matter of assent and trust. That is, both right and left hemispheres are involved. We have long recognized that conversion is not purely an intellectual response. Few love affairs have begun by reading a resumé. Often we feel, intuit, and experience something to be true before we understand it. If we teach only to the left brain, we are ignoring an important factor in faith development. Perhaps the point we are making can be better understood by looking at a particular life.

C. S. Lewis: Loving God with his whole mind

There is little question that C. S. Lewis is one of the 20th Century's most popular and influential Christian writers. It is a matter of debate whether this Oxford don has had a greater impact through his "left brain" books such as *Mere Christianity, Screwtape Letters,* and his powerful spiritual autobiography, *Surprised by Joy* or through his "right brain" stories and fantasies, such as *The Chronicles of Narnia*. Both areas of his writing have received a wide audience.

Before C. S. Lewis was able to love and serve God with his whole mind, an interior civil war had to be concluded. Before he could make his confession, both his imagination and his intellect had to be converted.

Clyde Staples Lewis was born in the winter of 1898 in Belfast, the second son born to a lawyer and a clergyman's daughter. When he was 10 he lost his mother to cancer and shortly after began to lose his father, not to death, but to grief and anger. Lewis took refuge in his imagination. He loved Beatrix Potter books and found even more enjoyment in creating a world called Animal-land. Later Animal-land became Boxen, which Lewis described in written stories that included a chronology and maps.

Though the family regularly attended church and he was taught to say his prayers, Lewis reports that in his childhood aesthetic experiences were rare and religious experiences occurred not at all. His early education took place in what Americans would call private boarding schools.

It was during this period that the two halves of his mind began to lead him in separate directions. In his early teen years, his rational mind was carefully honed in philosophy and language by his tutor, W. T. Kirkpatrick. This mind was completely pessimistic, believing the universe was "a rather regrettable institution."[3] Lewis concluded that there was "nothing in the universe to be obeyed and nothing to be believed except what was either comforting or exciting."[4] In another context Lewis wrote that during this period he not only maintained that God did not exist, but he was also very angry with God for not existing and was equally angry with God for creating a world.[5]

If the rational mind took him away from faith, the imaginative mind led him toward it, or to use his own terms, developed a desire for *Joy,* which he defined as an unsatisfied longing which itself is more desirable than any other satisfaction. Another time Lewis wrote that Joy was a longing that we feel for our "far-off country," "a longing which though painful, is felt to be somehow a delight. A hunger more satisfying than any other fullness; a poverty better than all other wealth. A desiring which, if long absent, is itself desired so much that the new desiring becomes an instance of the original one."[6]

Reflecting back on this period of his life, he later wrote that nothing short of a war had taken place between his imaginative life and the life of his intellect. "The two hemispheres of my mind were in the sharpest contrast. On the one side a many-islanded sea of poetry and myth; on the other a glib and shallow 'rationalism.' Nearly all that I loved I believed to be imaginary; nearly all that I believed to be real I thought grim and meaningless."[7]

In childhood Lewis had experienced Joy on several occasions. Once, while standing by a flowering currant bush, he remembered a time when his brother had brought a miniature toy garden into the nursery. The beauty of the bush and the memory of the toy garden produced in him a sensation of "Great Longing" or Joy. Later he understood that these experiences created a hunger for higher and higher experiences. If one faithfully pursued the experience of Joy one could ultimately realize that it cannot be met in things themselves. It finally led beyond oneself to the "Hidden Country," to Holiness.

The path to the hidden country, however, was still full of curves. Many places along the way claimed to be the final destination. Lewis discovered that though people long for Joy, they frequently settle for something less. "Sex is very often a substitute for Joy," he observed. "I sometimes wonder whether all pleasures are not substitutes for Joy."[8]

Other voices promised the experience of Joy, but could not deliver. He met magicians, spiritualists, and practitioners of the occult, but discovered that Joy did not point in those directions. Slowly he was being prepared for a powerful right-brained experience.

One day Lewis came upon a copy of *Phantastes, a Faerie Romance* by George MacDonald. These simple stories worked a powerful magic on him. It was the right book at the right time for the right brain. He was later to write that the book had about it "a cool, morning innocence, and also a certain quality of Death, good Death."[9]

This reading brought him back to his experience of Joy. It awakened within him a learning and yearning for Holiness. In his own words, "What it actually did to me was to convert, even to baptize my imagination. It did nothing to my intellect nor (at the time) to my conscience. Their turn came far later and with the help of many other books and men." [10]

Though the imagination had been baptized, the intellect had not. When he entered Oxford, Lewis considered himself an atheist—but he was an atheist under attack. "A young man who wishes to remain a sound Atheist cannot be too careful of his reading. There are traps everywhere—'Bibles laid open, millions of surprises,' as Herbert says, 'fine nets and stratagems.' God is, if I may say it, very unscrupulous." [11]

One by one the men he met and the authors he read battered away at the walls the intellect had erected to keep God out. Wham! Chesterton's essays beat on the wall. Wham! Bergson's philosophy battered the structure. Wham! Even the poetry of Herbert and Milton chipped away at his defenses. One day a firm atheist friend took a poke at the walls by confessing that the evidence for the historicity of the gospels was really surprisingly good. "Rum thing," he went on. "All that stuff of Frazer's about the Dying God. Rum thing. It almost looks as if it had really happened once." [12]

His close friends, including J. R. R. Tolkien, author of *The Hobbit*, helped him understand the relationship between story, myth, fairy tale, and Christianity. The final blow had struck his defenses, and, as in the battle of Jericho, his walls came tumbling down. One night he knelt in his room and prayed; he finally gave in to the love that would not let him go.

This first conversion was not final. It was a conversion to a belief in God—not the God of Jesus Christ. He still had not connected God and Joy. He read and thought and studied. He listened to arguments. His intellect worked overtime. Still, for all of the struggle and study, the final step toward Christianity was as much intuition as it was intellectual decision.

We will let the words of Lewis describe the actual event. "I know very well when, but hardly how, the final step was taken. I was driven to Whipsnade one sunny morning. When we set out I did not believe that Jesus Christ is the Son of God, and when we reached the zoo I did. Yet I had not exactly spent the journey in thought. Nor in great emotion . . . It was more like when a man, after long sleep, still lying motionless in bed, becomes aware that he is now awake." [13]

Storytelling—a whole-brain activity

We neither fall in love nor come to faith purely by means of rational assent. Still, many of our churches proceed as if the act of coming to faith is accomplished solely by receiving and processing information. When we tell the story of "The Prodigal Son"—or what may more accurately be called, "The Prodigal God"—the focus too often is on factual, or what some educators call *literal,* questions. "Now class, where did the younger son find work?" "What gifts did the father give his son when he returned home?" Literal questions certainly have a part to play in education, but they should never be the only questions asked. If our goal is not merely to make smarter children but to increase their faith, we must invite them to find their place in the biblical drama. "Are you more like the younger or older son?" "When the younger son returned home he expected to be treated like a servant, yet his father treated him like an honored child. Has anything similar ever happened to you?"

There are many ways to engage the right brain in learning. Art, music, dance, and storytelling—activities that excite the imagination—are great gifts to the church.

Storytelling is directed to the whole mind. As we hear and process the words through the left hemisphere, a series of images begins to form in the right hemisphere. When I tell the story of the healing of the paralyzed man (Mark 2:1-12), I frequently ask the listeners to describe what they "see." "Close your eyes," I say, "and focus on one scene in the story." After a few moments I ask the learners to share with another person what they have seen. Without exception the pictures they describe are vivid and detailed. If I ask further questions, "Imagine yourself in this story. Where are you in this story?" the responses are frequently illuminating and surprising.

When we hear a story told well, we naturally see it in our mind. The picture can be quickly lost, however, if the teacher directs all questions to the left hemisphere. "How many men did it take to carry the paralyzed man?" "What did the scribes do when they heard Jesus forgive the man's sins?" When the class is asked only to recall information, the vivid images are soon blurred or forgotten.

A teacher who wishes to encourage students to find connections with the story frequently will combine storytelling with other right hemisphere activities. Students will be asked to draw a picture of the story or play a part in a spontaneous drama. Walter Wink writes glowingly about his experiences with dance, body movement, and clay sculpture. "We must find ways to bring our whole selves to texts that are themselves the product of processes that involve both hemispheres."[14]

Preaching to the whole mind

In Andrew Greeley's study of Catholic young adults he concludes, "Ironically, while only a small percent rate the sermons as excellent, the sermon is the single most important parish activity in affecting the attitudes toward Catholicism. If sermons have any influence at all, it is a positive one." Later he writes, "Sermons have an independent influence of their own as strong as family and nature and Catholic schooling."[15]

Greeley's study says that even poor preaching is significant in the area of faith development. And remember, his study took place in a church that not too many years ago deemphasized preaching. Certainly the impact of the sermon in other churches must be equal or even greater.

If preaching is to have its full influence, it too must be directed to the whole mind. The goal of preaching is not just to inform, but to invite the listener to faith. One of the greatest aids in whole-brain preaching is storytelling. It excites the imagination as few left brain, three-point sermons can.

Jesus chose storytelling as his way of communicating. He told parables of the kingdom to kindle the imagination of his listeners and to help them envision something that was radically different from anything they had ever experienced. He helped them imagine a society where disagreements would be settled without force or the use of the secular court, where the role of the servant was the greatest office. It would be a community where barriers formed by race, gender, or nationality would be eliminated. A later disciple of Jesus summarized his teacher by writing, "There is neither Jew nor Greek, slave nor free, male nor female, for you are all one in Christ Jesus" (Gal. 3:28).

To communicate such a radical new vision of society, there needs to be a transformation of the whole mind. Jesus chose not to lecture on the subject but to convert the imagination by telling stories and parables. Does anyone doubt that storytelling was his most common and distinct way of teaching?

We who teach and proclaim have many different kinds of stories available for our use. First, of course, are the stories from Scripture. These sacred tales are the great treasury of the church. They are not simply stories of ancient people, they are stories of God, and, ultimately, our stories. As we listen to these stories we discover that we are both the prodigal and the younger sibling; we are the Levite, the priest, and the Samaritan who come across the wounded man on the Jericho road. When the story is told well, we find connections between our story and the story of God.

Another kind of story is the folktale, or fairy story. Tolkien and Lewis believed that stories, particularly the happily-ever-after-fairy-tale helped create a sense of wonder and awe, a sense of the marvelous or supernatural. They believed that the presence of the marvelous pulls us toward faith. It creates a hunger for the real thing, the fulfillment of all hungers. As we discovered in Lewis's life, story has the power to baptize the imagination, and to create a desire to experience that which is beyond our reach.[16]

The fairy story shares many characteristics with stories found in Scripture. Like New Testament stories, the fairy tale has a strong sense of virtue. It lives with the assurance that help is available when it is needed. Unlike the world, where people haven't got time for the pain, these stories teach that suffering should not be avoided. They teach that suffering even has power to transform our world.

Some observers have feared that the fairy story makes us live in a fantasy world. C.S. Lewis disagreed. "Far from dulling or emptying the actual world, [stories] give a new dimension of depth. The one who listens to stories does not despise real woods because he has read of enchanted woods. The reading makes all real woods a little enchanted."[17]

2

STORIES OF WORD AND WITNESS

The Student

This story, adapted from a piece by Anton Chekhov, speaks eloquently of the power of the biblical story. In the original story Chekhov wrote, "It was clear that what happened nineteen centuries ago still possesses a deep meaning for the present. . . ."

Ivan was caught miles from home when the temperature began to drop. He wore only a thin jacket and had nothing on his head to protect him from the cutting wind. A student at the theological seminary, he had taken this rare opportunity to go hunting while he was home on break for Holy Week. His fingers were numb and the wind burned his face.

"Good Friday weather has always been unpredictable," he thought as he searched the horizon for shelter. The only light he could see shone from the widow's gardens near the river. The village, where he lived, was hidden in the cold evening fog.

Oppressed by the cold, he fell to thinking that just such a

wind as this had blown in the time of Ivan the Terrible and Peter the Great. In those days people suffered from the same terrible poverty and hunger that crushed the lives of peasants now. People lived in the same ignorance, wretchedness, and desolation then, and a thousand years from now it would be no better. He did not want to go home.

The widow's gardens were called such because they were owned by two widows, a mother and daughter. A campfire was burning brightly, crackling and blazing in the night air. The widow Vasilisa, a tall, fat old woman in a man's coat was standing by and looking thoughtfully into the fire. Her daughter Lukerya, a little pock-marked woman, was sitting on the ground washing a kettle. They had just finished supper.

"Winter just won't go away," said the student walking up to the fire.

Vasilisa stared for a moment, until she remembered him. "I did not recognize you at first. God bless you."

As the women finished their chores they talked. Vasilisa had wonderful experiences to recount from her time as a nurse. Lukerya, who had suffered abuse from her husband, stared into space with no expression.

"The first Good Friday must have been cold like this," Ivan said, warming his hands over the flames. "St. Peter warmed himself by a fire. It was an extraordinarily long, sad night!"

He looked out at the darkness, shook his head, and continued. "No doubt you have attended a reading of the passion story."

"Yes, I have," Vasilisa answered.

"You remember at the Last Supper Peter said to Jesus, 'Lord, I am ready to go with you to prison and to death.' And the Lord answered, 'I tell you Peter, the cock will not crow this day, until you three times deny that you know me.' After the supper Jesus went through the agony of death in the garden, and prayed, but poor Peter was faint and weary, and his eyelids were heavy, and he could not win the struggle against sleep. So he slept. On that same night, as you know, Judas came and kissed Jesus and betrayed him to his tormentors. They bound him and took him to the high priest who beat him, while Peter, frazzled with anxiety and afraid that something terrible was about to happen, followed behind him. For Peter loved Jesus passionately, intensely, and now he could see them beating the one he loved."

Lukerya stopped cleaning the spoons and fixed her full attention on Ivan.

"They came to the house of the high priest," he continued, "where they began to interrogate Jesus. Meanwhile the workers made a fire in the yard because it was cold, and they warmed themselves. Peter stood near the fire with them and warmed himself as I am doing. A woman, who recognized him, said, 'He was with Jesus too,' suggesting that Peter should also be taken for interrogation. And all the workers must have turned and looked suspiciously, because Peter became flustered and said, 'I don't know him,' A little while later someone else recognized him as one of the disciples of Jesus and said, 'You also are one of them.' And again Peter denied it. Later, for a third time, someone turned to him: "Didn't I see you with him in the garden today?" for the third time Peter denied it, and immediately the cock crowed. Peter looked at Jesus far off and remembered the words he had said to him earlier in the evening. The Gospels say: 'He went out and wept bitterly.' And I imagine the garden was deathly silent except for the sound of his muffled sobbing."

Ivan sighed and looked out into the darkness. Vasilisa suddenly began to weep, and great tears flowed down her cheeks. She wiped her face, half embarrassed, on her sleeve, while her daughter, still gazing steadily at the student, grimaced as one who was suffering intense pain.

As the farm workers returned from the river, the light from the fire caught their faces. The student greeted them silently, then said good night to the two women and began his journey home. Again the darkness surrounded him, his fingers became numb and his face stung from the wind. It was hard to believe Easter was only two days away.

He thought about Vasilisa as he walked. Since she had cried when he told what happened to Peter the night before the crucifixion, the story must have had a special meaning for her.

He stopped and looked back at the fire. There was no one standing near it now. Both Vasilisa and her daughter were deeply moved by his words. The old woman had wept not because he was a great storyteller, but because it was a great story. Peter's life and her life were wound together.

Suddenly his soul was filled with joy, and for a moment he had to catch his breath. "The past," he thought, "is linked to the present by an unbroken chain of events which flow from one to the other." And it seemed to him that he had just seen both ends of that chain. When he touched one the other quivered.

As he crossed the river and mounted the hill Ivan thought about the power and beauty of the sacred story. It had been the story through which centuries of people had understood their lives. It was still the most powerful and wonderful truth on earth and now an inexpressible joy had taken possession of him and suddenly life was filled with deep meaning.

God Revealed

Adapted from a Jewish midrash.

When Moses and Aaron entered into the court of Pharaoh for the first time the normally busy and noisy room became silent. "Thus says the Lord, the God of Israel," Aaron announced in a ringing voice, " 'Let my people go!' "

"And who is this god who is giving orders?" the Pharaoh asked angrily. "What is his name? How many legions does God command?"

Moses and Aaron explained that the power of God has nothing to do with the way humans measure might. God does not need warriors. God's power can be seen in creation.

"God's name," the Pharaoh chided them, "you neglected to give me God's name."

"God's name is Yahweh. It was revealed to me through a burning bush," Moses explained.

"Ah," the Pharaoh said, "now we are getting someplace. Bring the books with the names of the gods."

The scribes of the Pharaoh brought out all of the chronicles of all the nations and searched the pages for the name of the God of Israel. In the books were the names of the gods of Sidon, and Moab, and Ammon, but they could not find the name of the God of Israel.

Moses and Aaron explained, "The names of the gods you find in the book are dead gods. Our God, the God of Israel, is a living God!"

The Pharaoh remained unconvinced. "I don't know your God. I have never heard of your God and I will not obey any god I do not know."

Soon the Pharaoh learned to know the God of Moses and Aaron through a series of unique revelations—the plagues of frogs, gnats, flies, boils, hail, locusts, darkness, and, ultimately, the death of the firstborn. He knew God through punishment.

The Proper Preparation

A student approached the Teacher and announced that he was ready to assume the office of the ministry.

"And what are your qualifications?" the Teacher asked.

"I have mastered the art of physical discipline," the student replied. "I am able to sleep on the ground, to eat nothing but raw grains, and I can carry huge loads on my back."

The Teacher took the young man by the arm and led him

toward a field. "Do you see that mule? He too sleeps on the ground, eats nothing but grains, and can bear large burdens on his back. Up to this point you may qualify to be an ass, but you are not yet ready for the ministry."

The Fourth Temptation

Satan, the great deceiver, was about to lecture some of his young recruits on the fine art of deception. "Before I begin," he said, "I would like to hear what you consider to be the best methods of leading people away from God."

"I think the best method is to convince people that there is no God," said the youngest of the recruits.

"We call your method, 'The Frontal Attack,' " Satan commented. "It has been used for centuries without great success. Only a handful of people ever accept a true position of atheism."

"Perhaps we could convince people that there is no hell," a second recruit suggested.

Satan sighed, "That was very successful for a long period of time. Liberals liked that line of reasoning very much. Unfortunately, we have promoted so much hatred and war that now people sense that they will have to account for all the evil they do."

A small recruit ventured a suggestion, "Rather than try to convince people that there is no God, we should plant the idea that God is so easy-going that there is no need in making an immediate decision."

"Ah," the great deceiver said grimly, "You have stumbled on our second most effective temptation. Procrastination! For centuries it has been our best method with the young. Its only serious defect is that it is ineffective with older people."

"Then what is the best method of deception," the recruits all asked eagerly.

"Our best method works with those who go to church regularly as well as those who do not. We call it 'Moderation.' We convince people not to get too excited or fanatical about God. This way they convince themselves they are believers though in truth there is no fire in the soul. 'Moderation' works just about every time."

The Letter

The friends of Jesus know very little about the future except that one day we will be together, just as he promised.

Before a young man left for a long journey he handed a letter to the woman he intended to marry. "It is a pledge of my honor and love," the young man assured her.

Days turned into months and months into years, but the young woman never heard from her beloved. As time passed she became more and more depressed. The young woman's friends urged her to forget the traveler and to begin to see other men. She steadfastly refused.

One day while looking through her desk she discovered the letter her beloved had left her. She read it slowly and her spirits lifted. In the days ahead she read and reread the letter many times. It gave her great comfort.

Finally, after many years, the young man returned home. "I am grateful, but amazed, that you are still waiting for me. How was it possible for you to remain faithful during my long absence?" he asked.

"Even you don't understand?" the young woman said. "I believed in you because I had your word, in the letter."

The Three Thieves

This story is told in Ethiopia to remind people they must know what they stand for, and they must not listen to the voices of the world, no matter how convincing those voices sound.

There was once a man who had a pet lamb. He fed it by hand and played with it every day. When hard times came he was forced to take his pet lamb to market, to sell it.

Now there were three thieves who heard of the man's plan and plotted to take the lamb from him in a unique way.

Early in the morning the man rose and put the lamb over his shoulders, to carry it to market. As he traveled down the road the first thief approached him and said, "Why are you carrying that dog on your shoulders?"

The man laughed, "This is not a dog. It is my pet lamb. I am taking it to market," he said.

After he walked a bit further the second thief crossed his path and said, "What a fine looking dog you have. Where are you taking it?"

Puzzled, the man took the lamb off his shoulders and looked carefully at it. "This is not a dog," he said slowly. "It is a lamb and I am taking it to market."

Shortly before he reached the market the third thief met the man and said, "Sir, I don't think that they will allow you to take your dog into the market."

Completely confused, the man took the lamb off his shoulders and set it on the ground. "If three different people say that this is a dog, then surely it must be a dog," he thought. He left the lamb behind and walked to the market. If he had bothered to turn around he would have seen the three thieves picking up the lamb and going toward their home.

Columba

The Irish people have always loved stories. They have also loved their storytellers, the bards, who traveled throughout the country telling tales, memorized word for word, and singing old songs. If the bards were angered by the way they were treated or unhappy with their pay, they often made up songs and stories that ridiculed their opponents.

In sixth century Ireland, there lived a giant monk who was a friend of the bards. The son of a powerful chieftain, Columba had studied under a famous bard. Though he loved oral stories, Columba loved written stories even more. The problem was that few books existed in Ireland during the sixth century. Most of the books were to be found in monasteries.

In order to satisfy his hunger for reading, Columba, wearing a horsehair shirt, walked from monastery to monastery reading every book he could find. It was not enough for Columba to just read a book, however. He attempted to copy every book he read.

Although many monks greeted their giant friend with genuine warmth, others were jealous of their books. They refused to allow Columba to copy their books, preferring to possess the only copy.

One day Columba, accompanied by his pet crane, went to visit his friend Finian who had just returned from Rome with a new book. Finian welcomed Columba to his monastery and invited him to read the new book, but insisted that he not copy it.

Columba agreed to the terms, but as he read the book he was so captivated by its content that he was determined to have his own copy. For several nights he crept into the library with his inks and pens and copied the entire book. Just as he completed the task Finian discovered his friend at work. A great argument arose in which each man claimed to be the owner of the second book. Unable to settle their dispute, they went before the king of Ireland who acted as the judge.

In the end the king ruled in Finian's favor declaring that "Every calf belongs to the cow." The copy belonged to the original owner.

Columba was outraged and vowed revenge. He returned to his father's tribe and convinced them to support him in a war against the king. The army quickly handed the king a terrible defeat in which three thousand of the royal soldiers lay dead while but a single man died who fought for Columba.

When the war was over, rather than rejoicing in his triumph, Columba felt remorse. The cost of revenge had been too dear. More than three thousand men were dead to satisfy his anger. He had not acted in accord with his Lord's desires.

As an act of penance, Columba vowed never to lay eyes on his beloved Ireland again. In 563 he went into voluntary exile, sailing north with a handful of companions to Iona, an island, just off the coast of Scotland.

Once on Iona, Columba and his friends built a small village. They then crisscrossed all of Iona and Scotland preaching and starting new churches. Even the king of Scotland was converted.

Of course each church must have a Bible. So Columba made three hundred copies of the New Testament in order that all would have access to the story of Jesus.

One day, when Columba had lived on Iona for 28 years, a fleet of Irish boats sailed into the harbor. Ninety men, bishops, priests, and deacons, had arrived to tell Columba of the terrible fight that had taken place between the bards and the king. The bards had demanded money from the king and threatened to sing songs to disgrace him if he refused. The king retaliated by banishing the bards from Ireland. What would Ireland be without its storytellers?

"Columba," they said, "you must return and settle the dispute for no one else has credibility with both sides."

"I cannot go," Columba insisted, "I have made a vow never to set my eyes on Ireland again." Still the situation was not simple and he wrestled for days until he found a solution. He had vowed not to look at Ireland, but his vow did not include stepping on Irish soil.

Columba sailed back to Ireland with a blindfold over his eyes. Back in his beloved country he was greeted as a returning hero. They looked with wonder on the figure that had not bent with the years and listened with awe at his still powerful voice.

Day after day Columba met with the bards and king separately. Then he brought them together. Finally, the bards agreed to live by the rules and the king allowed them to stay. Columba returned to Iona knowing that he had a hand in saving the art of storytelling in Ireland. Six years later he died at his desk, copying a new book.

Hitting the Bullseye

This Jewish tale contains some excellent advice on the art of storytelling.

There was once a rabbi who answered every question by telling a story. One day a student asked his teacher, "Rabbi, you have a wonderful ability to select just the right story for each question. What is your secret?"

Smiling impishly, the old teacher replied, "That reminds me of a story. Once a young soldier was traveling through the country when he stopped to rest his horse in a small village. As he walked around the small houses he spotted a wood fence. On the wood fence were nearly forty small chalk circles and right in the center of each was a bullet hole.

What amazing accuracy, the soldier thought as he examined the fence. *There is not a single shot that has not hit the bullseye.*

The soldier quickly set out to find the one who possessed such great skill. He was told that the sharpshooter was a small boy.

"Who taught you to shoot so well?" the soldier asked.

"I taught myself," the young lad replied.

Not yet satisfied the soldier pressed the young boy, "To what do you contribute your great skill?"

"Actually," the young lad began, "it is not very difficult. First I shoot at the wall, and then I take a piece of chalk and draw circles around the holes."

The rabbi chuckled for a moment. "Now you know my secret. I don't look for a story to answer a question. I collect every good story or parable I hear and then store it in my mind. When the right occasion or question arises, I point the story in its direction. In effect, I simply draw a circle around a hole that is already there."

Find Your Own Story

A woman came to the Teacher and shared her great sorrow in life, "I have been married nearly a dozen years and I have not yet given birth to a child."

"What are you willing to do about it?" the Teacher asked.

The woman did not know what to say.

"My mother," the Teacher told her, "was aging and still had no child. Then she heard that a great holy man was visiting a nearby town on his way home from a teaching mission. She hurried to his inn and begged him to pray that she might bear a son. 'What are you willing to do about it?' he asked.

" 'My husband is a poor bookbinder,' she replied, 'but I do have one fine thing that I can give to you.' She went home as fast as she could and fetched her good cape, which was carefully stored away in a chest.

"But when she returned to the inn with it, the Teacher had already left for the next town. My mother immediately set out after him and since she had no money to ride, she walked from town to town with her cape until she found him. The Holy Man took the cape and hung it on the wall. 'It is acceptable,' he said. My mother walked all the way back, until she reached home. A year later I was born."

"I will do like your mother," cried the woman. "I will bring you a good cape of mine, so that I may get a son."

"That won't work," said the Teacher. "You heard the story. My mother had no story to go by."

The Chosen People

Although I have heard this story told several times, I have been unable to locate a written source.

The Lord God decided to select a nation to be his chosen people. First he interviewed the Greeks. "If I was to be your God and you were to be my people, what could you do for me?" the Lord asked.

"O Lord," the Greek people replied, "if you were to be our God and we were to be your people we would honor you with the finest art and the loftiest systems of thought. Our great thinkers would extol you in their great writings."

"Thank you for your offer," the Lord said.

Next God visited the Romans. "If I were to be your God and you were to be my people, what could you do for me?"

"Great king of the universe," the Romans said, "we are a nation of builders. If you were to be our God and we were to be your people we would erect great buildings in your name and wonderful road systems so that your people could travel to worship in these great buildings."

The Lord seemed pleased with the offer, and thanked the Romans.

From Rome the Lord went all over the world, interviewing one nation after another. Finally, he interviewed a small Mideastern group, the Jews, who had a reputation for being shrewd traders.

Once again the Lord asked his question. "If I was to be your God and you were to be my people, what could you do for me?"

"Lord," the Jewish people said, "we are not known for our power or our art or our buildings. However, we are a nation of storytellers. If you were to be our God and we were to be your children, we could tell your story throughout the whole world."

God, who also had a reputation for being a shrewd trader, said, "It's a deal!"

A Special Storyteller

This story is often repeated by the growing number of storytellers in the United States to emphasize one of the strengths of storytelling, its intimacy.

People in an African village purchased a television set. For weeks all of the children and all of the adults gathered around the set morning, afternoon, and night watching the programs. Then after a couple of months the set was turned off and never used again.

A visitor to the village asked the chief, "Why do you no longer watch television?"

"We have decided to listen to the storytellers," he replied.

"Doesn't the television know more stories?" the visitor asked.

"Yes," the chief replied, "but the storyteller knows me."

3

STORIES OF FAITH AND FAITHFULNESS

The Stray Lamb

This story is based on a Jewish folktale and Luke 15:4-7.

When Moses was forced to flee Egypt he went to the land of Midian, where he found a job tending sheep for a man named Jethro. Moses was a good shepherd, spending his days tending and caring for his flock. He knew each sheep and each lamb and could call them by name.

Often when he was in the fields Moses would dream of his days in the court of the Egyptian pharaoh. He remembered the splendor, the soft beds, the royal feasts. At times the memories seemed like they belonged to someone else.

Moses also remembered his people living in bondage, oppressed by the cruel Egyptian slave drivers. He longed for the day when

God would free them and lead them back to their own country, the land of Israel.

One day Moses led his flock of 100 sheep across the desert to the foot of Mt. Sinai, a forbidding mountain whose rocks were razor sharp. In the flat land, at the foot of the mountain, however, the sheep were free to eat peacefully. When it grew dark Moses counted the sheep before leading them home. He discovered that one, perhaps the smallest lamb, was missing. Looking around, he found tiny hoofprints leading toward the mountain.

Should he lead the 99 back to Jethro's home, or should he temporarily abandon the flock and search for the one lost lamb? Though each decision was fraught with danger, he could not bear the thought of abandoning that tiny lamb.

Leaving the 99 Moses raced up the side of the mountain, following the hoofprints as best he could. All night long he searched, looking behind every rock. Finally, toward morning, he found the trembling lamb, weak and frightened. He lifted it to his shoulders rejoicing, and headed back down the mountain.

It was nearly dawn when he arrived at the foot of the mountain. Suddenly he saw an eerie sight. A bush was on fire, but the flame did not consume it. Then he heard a voice that came from the bush, "Moses, Moses!"

"Here I am," he said.

"Do not come near. Take off your shoes, for the place where you are standing is holy ground. Moses, I am the God of Abraham, the God of Isaac, and the God of Jacob."

And Moses hid his face, for he was afraid to look at God.

"Moses," the voice continued, "just as you have saved this stray lamb, I have chosen you to save my flock, the Children of Israel, from slavery in Egypt. You shall go to the Pharaoh and tell him to let my people go. One day, after you lead my flock out of Egypt, you will worship me upon this mountain."

All this time Moses held the stray lamb on his shoulders. As he put the lamb on the ground he realized that he was being called to carry Israel on his shoulders out of slavery to the promised land.

Idolatry

"I am the Lord your God, who brought you out of Egypt, out of the land of slavery. You shall have no other gods before me."   Exodus 20:2-3

"Why," the heathen king, Rufus, asked the Teacher, "do your people grow so angry with us?"

"First," the Teacher said, "let me tell you that I recently received two new dogs. I named them Rufus and Rufina, after you and your wife, the queen."

"How dare you insult my wife and me by sharing our beloved names with your dogs," the king thundered. "Have you no respect for either of us?"

"I don't understand your anger," the Teacher said calmly. "Both you and the dogs are created by God. Both of you eat and drink, bring forth offspring, and die. Yet you grow indignant when you discover you share your name with a dog. Please note that God, who stretched forth the heavens and laid the foundations of the earth, is the Creator of all animate and inanimate things. Yet you make an idol of wood and stone, worship it, and call it by the name of God. Now do you understand why we get so angry with you?"

The Fourth Talent

This story is based on Matthew 25:14-30.

Once there was a businessman who entrusted his property to his employees. To one servant he gave $5,000, to a second

$2,000, and a third $1,000. The first two invested the money and returned 100 cents on the dollar, while the third employee buried the money in the earth. On the day of accounting he returned the original money to the master and was soundly chastised for failing to invest wisely.

A fourth employee was given $3,000 to invest. He returned several days after the accounting took place and approached the master cautiously. "I invested the money that you left with me," he confessed, "but the investment turned sour. Not only has your money gained no interest, I have lost nearly $1,000 of the amount you entrusted to me."

The master smiled at his worried servant. "Well done, good and faithful servant. You invested as you were commanded. You have been faithful over a little, I will set you over much."

The Old Man and the Tree

When asked what he would do if he knew the world was going to end tomorrow, Martin Luther said, "Go out and plant a tree." He may have been quoting from this Jewish midrash.

The emperor was riding toward Tiberias when he saw a very old man digging in the earth to plant trees. "Old man," the emperor shouted, "Surely you don't expect to eat the fruit of the trees you are planting."

"I have not given up that hope," the old man answered. "While I have strength I will do my duty."

"How old are you?" the emperor inquired.

"I am a 100 years old," the planter said. "God, who granted me longevity, may even allow me to eat of the fruit of these trees. But in any case when I plant trees I am merely imitating God's act of creation when he ordered that the earth bring forth fruit-bearing trees" (Gen. 1:11).

"Promise me," the emperor said, "that if you are alive when these trees bear figs you will let me know."

Several years later when the trees produced fruit the old man loaded a basket full of figs and made his way to the king's palace. When he arrived at the gate he was initially refused admission, but due to his persistence and his old age, he was granted an audience with the king.

"I am the old man you saw planting trees several years ago," he told the emperor. "I have brought a basket full of figs which I plucked from the trees you saw me planting."

So pleased was the emperor with his gift that he accepted the fruit and ordered that the basket be filled with coins. Then he addressed the old man, "Go home, good friend, and continue to participate with almighty God in the act of creation."

The Most Valuable Thing in the House

Another version of this story can be found in my book, Stories for Telling. *I have included this version because it is shorter, and perhaps more usable.*

A man came to his rabbi and said, "Since my marriage of 10 years has produced no children, I ask that you grant me a letter of divorce from my wife."

The wise rabbi, knowing his friend to be an impulsive man, urged him to go home and make a sort of feast in commemoration of the coming event. "I see no reason," the Rabbi said, "why a divorce should not be celebrated in some way, similar to marriage."

The man, who was willing to do almost anything to stay in the rabbi's good graces, went home and gave a banquet. As he ate and drank his spirits soared. "Wife," he said, "I am prepared to let you take the most valuable thing in the house with you as a sign of my good faith. I wish you long years and happiness."

After the guests went home, the man, tired from drinking and celebrating, fell into a deep sleep. The woman quickly ordered her servants to carry him to her father's house. When he awoke the next morning, finding himself in a strange house, he demanded an explanation.

"I am only acting upon your word," the wife said softly. "Last evening you offered me the most precious thing in the house. You, dear husband, are of far more value than any item of furniture."

The man was deeply touched by his wife's affection. The next day he again approached his rabbi. "My wife and I have come to ask your prayers on our behalf, so that the Lord will grant us heirs."

The rabbi assured the man that he had already begun to pray for the two of them. Nine months later the woman gave birth to their first child.

Three Deaths

This is yet another story whose roots are in Jewish oral history.

A man was engaged to a woman who often told lies. Though the man implored her to tell the truth, she did not give up the vicious practice.

One day the young woman told her fiancé that his father had made several advances toward her. He found the story too incredible to believe but she insisted it was true. She continued with this story for many weeks. Finally, the woman told him to come to her house unannounced the next evening and he could see for himself.

Arriving at the house, he found his father in a kneeling posture before the woman, begging her to give up her slanderous habits. The young man, however, seeing his father's posture and not able to hear his words, believed that the situation affirmed his beloved's accusations. In a moment of rage he killed his father. In the ensuing investigation the woman admitted that she had slandered the dead man. The authorities ordered that the son be put to death for murder and the woman suffer the same penalty, for being the chief cause of the whole tragedy. Thus, the word of the great teachers were sadly reinforced: "Slander has three victims: the slanderer, the victim, and the hearer."

The Magic Seeds

A thief was sentenced to death by hanging for stealing a small package of meat. Before he was taken to the gallows he was allowed to address the king. "Your majesty," the thief said humbly, "I am the only man living who knows how to plant an apple seed that will grow and bear fruit overnight. To atone for my crime I would like to teach you and your court the secret. I will need a shovel, a handful of apple seeds, and a maiden who has not tasted love's first kiss."

Eagerly the king, his 13-year-old daughter, and all his advisors gathered in an open field to learn this most wonderful secret. In the most elaborate manner possible, bowing and making dramatic gestures, the thief dug a small hole. "Now," the thief said, "the water must be poured in the hole by this tender maiden."

The king's daughter stepped forward and carefully poured a small container of water in the freshly dug hole.

"We are ready for the actual planting," the thief said addressing the assembled group. "The seed can only be placed in the earth by someone who has never taken a single item that did not belong to them, no matter how small or how long ago."

"I would like to have my most trusted advisor, the prime

minister, be the one who plants this magic seed in the ground," the king announced.

Hesitating, the prime minister said meekly, "I am afraid that I am not eligible, your majesty. When I was young I took a jacket that was not mine."

"Perhaps it is best that our loyal treasurer be the one to plant the seed," the king said quickly.

"Majesty," the treasurer said with some embarrassment, "you forget that in a previous position I foolishly kept a small amount of money that did not rightfully belong to me."

One by one the king's advisors coughed, sputtered, and explained meekly that they were not able to plant the seed. Finally, even the king admitted that he once took a small item that belonged to his father.

When each had spoken the thief addressed the king. "The members of your court are men and women of the highest ethical standards. They are recognized as devoted public servants, yet not one of them can say they have never taken something that did not belong to them. How is it that I am to be hanged for taking a bit of food?"

"You are a wise and crafty man," the king said to the thief. "I now give you a full and complete pardon."

Lost and Found

This is but one of a whole collection of stories of Nasrudin, the wise fool. These mideastern stories come out of the Moslem tradition.

Nasrudin moved through the streets of his village saying, "My donkey is missing. Whoever returns it will receive the donkey as a reward."

People shook their heads and told Nasrudin, "You are making no sense."

"Quite the contrary," Nasrudin countered. "If the donkey is returned I will experience life's two greatest pleasures: finding something treasured that was lost, and giving away something that is highly valued."

The Rabbi and the Sick Man

Jewish folklore teaches that doing justice and providing mercy supersede any of the commandments, even commandments about the Sabbath.

Late one Friday afternoon, a rabbi was walking swiftly toward his village, carrying a bundle full of valuable items. "If all goes well" he thought, "I will reach home before the Sabbath begins."

Suddenly he heard a voice crying, "Rabbi, please help me. I am unable to walk. Help me reach the village."

For a moment, terror gripped the rabbi's heart. If he carried the man, thus obeying the commandment of God, he would have to leave his bundle, for he could not carry both. Without the bundle he could not care for his wife and children, which is also a commandment. Should he carry the man or his family's food into the village?

His indecision lasted for just a moment. How could he leave the man? He set the bundle down, lifted up the sick man, and carried him slowly into the village. He took the man to his own home, found him a place to rest, and then ran back where he left his bundle. As he headed back to his village he realized that for the first time in his life he would be breaking the Sabbath by traveling. It was also the first time that he has neglected his family.

As the rabbi rushed through the village gates and down the streets he heard voices at the windows saying, "Can you imagine, our rabbi is walking around with his bundle on the Sabbath. A Sabbath-breaker!"

In remorse the rabbi prayed, "If I have broken the Sabbath, God forgive me!"

Suddenly sunshine flooded the sky and the whole village was awash with light. The rabbi heard a voice, "My dear servant, you put a stranger's needs before your own. Go home, eat your bread, drink your wine, for I have lengthened the day. The Sabbath still awaits you.

And the voice said, "The Sabbath was made for man, not man for the Sabbath."

In Confidence

This wonderful Jewish story has had special meaning in our congregation where we have trained people to be lay caring ministers. Confidentiality is vital because it is key to building trust.

The Teacher and one of his companions made a house call on a rich man. They were seeking funds for a man who had suffered a severe heart attack.

The host greeted the Teacher and his friend warmly and listened intently as the Teacher briefly described the desperate plight of the one who had suffered the ailment. "We are asking you for a generous gift," the Teacher concluded.

"Who is the sick man?" the host asked.

The Teacher shook his head. "Rarely do we reveal the name of people in need. In this case it is most difficult for the man to admit that he needs charity."

"If I am to help I insist on knowing the identity of the man in need. I will keep it in strictest confidence. I was going to give you $500, but if you tell me the man's name I will increase the gift to $1,000."

"We will not reveal the man's name," the Teacher said shaking his head.

"Two thousand dollars. Surely you will not refuse such an amount."

"I will not break confidence," the Teacher insisted. His friend looked at his mentor in disbelief.

Taking a deep breath the host said, "Three thousand dollars."

Before the Teacher could reply his companion pleaded with him. "Teacher, three thousand dollars will pay for all the hospital and living expenses. He is an honorable man; he can keep the secret with us."

The Teacher walked toward the door, "I should have left long ago. The honor of a man is not open to barter or negotiation regardless of what the sum of money might be. I have other visits to make."

Before he could leave the house the rich man begged the Teacher to meet with him privately in the next room. The moment they were alone he broke into tears. "Teacher, I recently lost every penny I saved. I am not able to even make a token payment on the mortgage. I have wanted to go to someone for help, but I couldn't stand the idea of everyone in the city knowing that I am a failure."

"Now I understand," the Teacher said tenderly. "You were testing me to see if I could be trusted with your secret. I will seek funds for you as well as the man who is sick. What you have told me will be kept in confidence."

The two men bid their host farewell and walked toward the place of their next visit. "Well, Teacher," his friend said, "how much did he give you?"

The Teacher smiled and then playfully shook a finger at his friend. "Shame on you. You know such things are a secret."

4

STORIES OF
LOVE AND
FORGIVENESS

The Crown of Creation

The origin of this story is found in Jewish oral tradition.

When God had nearly finished with the act of creation, an announcement was made that the only thing left was to create a creature capable of understanding and marveling in the greatness of God. This being, called human, was not only to be of the earth, like all other creatures, but also to be created in the image of God. "Let these beings have reason, intellect, and understanding," God declared.

Truth then approached the Almighty pleading, "Oh God, I ask you to refrain from calling into being a creature who is capable of lying. The last thing we need is to have a world filled with deception and fraud."

Peace came forth to support this petition. "O Lord, I beg you not to create creatures who will disturb the harmony of your creation. I fear that these humans will act with revenge and initiate war."

While they were pleading against the creation of man, the soft voice of Charity asked to be heard. "Dear God, I know that any being created in your likeness will have the capacity to perform great and kind deeds. Filled with your Spirit these human beings will comfort the sick, visit the lonely, and provide shelter to the homeless. Such a being cannot but bring glory to you, O Lord."

Though God listened to the voice of Truth and Peace before the final act of creation, it was because of Charity that human beings were created.

The Same Kind of Folks

This story is based on an American folktale.

A farmer was working in his field when a stranger approached him. The traveler asked, "What kind of people live in the next town?"

Without pausing from his work the farmer replied, "What kind of people lived in the town you just left?"

"They were horrible," the traveler said waving his hand for emphasis. "People were dishonest, selfish, and inconsiderate."

Looking up, the farmer shook his head, "I'm sorry to say that's probably what you'll find in this town, too."

The stranger moaned and walked away.

Late in the same day another man happened down the same road. When he saw the farmer he called out, "What kind of people live in this next town?"

Without looking up the farmer returned with a question, "What kind of people lived in the town you just left?"

"They were thoughtful, friendly, and kind," the traveler beamed. "I hated to leave them."

The farmer put down his hoe, extended his hand and smiled. "I'm pleased to say that is about how you'll find folks here," he said.

The traveler returned the smile, shook the farmer's hand and headed toward his new home.

Leaking Sins

This story, which appears to be based on Luke 6:41-42, comes from the Desert Fathers.

One of the men in the community committed a serious sin. The council called a meeting and requested the Teacher to attend. When he refused to come they sent a delegation telling him the matter was most urgent. "Since you insist," he said, "I will come in about 30 minutes."

When he arrived at the meeting of the council, the Teacher entered the room carrying a leaking jug on his back, filled with water. The members of the council asked, "Teacher, what is this?"

"All day long," the Teacher replied, "my sins run out behind me and I am unaware of them. Yet despite my blindness to my own sin, today I am asked to judge the error of another."

When they heard the words of the Teacher they forgave the man who had sinned and said no more.

Carrying a Friend

See Mark 2:1-12

"What is your favorite Bible story, papa?" the little girl asked her father as he tucked her under the sheets.

"Let me see," he said as he sat on the edge of the bed. "There are so many that I love. The story we read tonight at supper of the four men who carried their paralyzed friend to Jesus, lowering him through the roof, is one of my favorites because it reminds me so much of how your uncle Hans was healed."

"I don't know that story," the little girl said hopefully. "Please tell it to me, papa."

"Many years ago," the father began, "Hans and his wife, Enid, escaped the war in Europe so that he could continue his life of teaching in the seminary. At first things were difficult because his English was not good, but soon he became one of our seminary's most beloved teachers. The students loved him because he was warm and gentle and when he spoke the Scriptures came alive.

"Hans and Enid were very much in love. Nearly every day they took long walks together, holding hands. It warmed the hearts of students and faculty alike to see them sitting close to each other in church.

"Then one day Enid died. Hans was struck with sorrow. For weeks he would not eat or take walks. The seminary president, along with three other friends, visited him regularly, but he felt lonely and depressed. He was experiencing the dark night of the soul.

"On one of their visits, Hans said to his friends, 'I am no longer able to pray to God. In fact, I am not certain I believe in God.'

"After a moment of silence, the seminary president said, 'Then we will believe for you. We will make your confession for you. We will pray for you.'

"The other friends looked bewildered by their president's words, but not knowing what else to say, they agreed.

"In the days ahead the four men met daily for prayer. They made confession on behalf of Uncle Hans. They asked God to restore the gift of faith to their dear friend and they continued to visit him in his home.

"Then, after many months, the four men all gathered in Hans's living room. He smiled before he spoke. 'It is no longer necessary for you to pray for me. Today, I would like you to pray with me.'

"The dark night of the soul had passed."

There was a long silence before the little girl spoke. "Uncle Hans was just like the sick man in the story, wasn't he, papa? Only instead of a pallet to carry him to Jesus, his friends used prayer."

The father nodded and kissed his daughter.

Two Natures

The Teacher sat praying under a tree that had large, exposed roots. As he prayed a scorpion, hanging on one of the roots, began to move slowly toward him. A young boy passing by saw the scorpion only inches away from the one in prayer and shouted, "Teacher, quick, kill that scorpion; it is trying to bite you!"

The Teacher looked up at the scorpion and slowly moved a short distance before he spoke to the lad, "Just because it is the nature of the scorpion to sting is no reason that I should change my nature to save."

How God Spoke to St. Francis through Brother Leo

The next two stories are but a small part of the legendary tales that surround the life of St. Francis of Assisi.

Once St. Francis and Brother Leo were staying together and found that they had no breviary with which to say matins. Francis decided to improvise and so said to Brother Leo, "I will say like this, 'Oh, Brother Francis, you have done so much evil and sin in the world that you deserve hell.' You, Brother Leo, shall answer: 'It is true that you deserve the depths of hell.' It is very important that you repeat this phrase without changing a word."

Brother Leo, who was as simple and pure as a man could be replied, "All right, father. Begin in the name of the Lord."

St. Francis began, "Oh, Brother Francis, you have done so many evil deeds and sins in the world that you deserve hell."

And Brother Leo answered: "God will perform so much good through you that you will go to paradise."

St. Francis was quite upset. "Don't say that, Brother Leo! Answer exactly like this, 'You certainly deserve to be placed among the damned.' "

"I will do as you say," Brother Leo replied.

Then, beating his breast, St. Francis cried, "Oh, my Lord, I have committed so many evil deeds and sins against you that I deserve to be utterly damned."

Brother Leo answered: "Oh, Brother Francis, God will make you such that you will be remarkably blessed among the blessed."

"Why don't you answer as I have told you?" St. Francis scolded. "Under holy obedience I command you to say, 'You are not worthy of finding mercy.' "

"Go ahead, father," Leo said meekly. "This time I will say just what you tell me."

Kneeling down and lifting up his head, St. Francis prayed sadly, "Oh, Brother Francis, do you think God will have mercy on you, for you have committed so many sins?"

But Brother Leo answered, "God the Father, whose mercy is infinitely greater than your sins, will be merciful to you and grant you grace."

St. Francis was angry and said to Brother Leo, "Why have you dared to go against my wishes and to answer the opposite of what I told you?"

Then Brother Leo replied gently and humbly, "God knows,

dear father, that each time I resolved in my heart to answer as you told me, but God makes me speak as pleases him and not as pleases me. Dear father, try as I do, the only words that God gives me are ones of grace and forgiveness. I can't say anything else because God is speaking through my mouth."

St. Francis and the Wolf of Gubbio

Perhaps all the stories and legends of St. Francis can be classified under the topic of love. For Francis's love and forgiveness are directed to all creation, not just the human family.

Francis loved animals of all kinds. Travel after a rain was extremely slow because Francis stopped and picked up worms along the path in order not to step on them. He fed and named the mice that lived in his monastic cell. It is said that the larks all sang to him on the night of his death.

Perhaps the most famous animal in the life of Francis was a wolf that terrified the people in the town of Gubbio. This wolf killed other animals and even devoured human beings. Though no one traveled without carrying a weapon, they found that their primitive clubs and spears were no match for the sharp teeth of the wolf.

One day St. Francis made a visit to Gubbio. Upon arrival the citizens warned him about the wolf. "Don't go outside the gate, Brother Francis," they said, "because the wolf will attack and kill you!"

Francis said to the people, "Jesus Christ is the Lord of all creatures." Then, without a shield, helmet, or weapon, he and a companion walked out into the country. A few peasants followed him from a distance. Others climbed trees and stood on roof tops to view the encounter between Francis and the wolf.

Soon the wolf appeared. When he saw Francis he broke into a

run with his mouth open. Francis made the sign of the cross and called out, "Brother Wolf, in the name of Christ I order you not to hurt me or anyone."

As soon as Francis made the sign of the cross the wolf closed its terrible jaws and stopped running. When Francis ordered the wolf to come to him, it lowered its head and lay down at the saint's feet, as though it had become a lamb.

"Brother Wolf," Francis said, "you have done great harm in this region and you have committed horrible crimes by destroying God's creatures without any mercy. You have killed human beings who have been created in the image of God. You deserve to be treated like a murderer and be put to death. This whole town is your enemy. But, Brother Wolf, I want to make peace between you and the people of Gubbio."

The wolf indicated by moving his body that he was willing to accept the saint's judgment.

Francis continued, "Brother Wolf, since you are willing to keep the peace, I promise that the people of this town will feed you each day so that you need never suffer from hunger again, for I know that whatever you have been doing is because you are very hungry. At the same time, Brother Wolf, I want you to promise you will never again hurt any animal or human being. Do you promise?"

The wolf nodded its head, promising to do what the saint asked.

"Now Brother Wolf," Francis concluded, "I want you to give me a sign of your pledge. The saint held out his hand and the wolf raised its front paw and gently placed it in St. Francis's hand as a sign of its pledge.

Then the wolf followed St. Francis into town like a gentle lamb. People gathered in amazement to see the strange sight. Francis gave a wonderful sermon in which he said that the fires of hell were much more dangerous than the powers of a wolf. He told them that the wolf had pledged to be peaceful as long as they fed him. Once again the wolf raised its right paw and put it in St. Francis's hand as a pledge.

Both the people of Gubbio and the wolf kept the pact that Francis made. The wolf went door to door for food and hurt no one. People fed it courteously and it is said that not a single dog barked at it.

Two years later the wolf died. The people of Gubbio mourned the loss of their new friend because the wolf's peaceful nature and patience reminded them of the virtues and holiness of St. Francis.

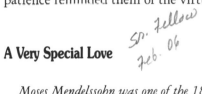

A Very Special Love

Moses Mendelssohn was one of the 18th century's most brilliant thinkers. The son of a poor scribe, Mendelssohn's pioneering scholarship was acclaimed by both Jewish and Christian teachers throughout Germany. Though himself an observant Jew, several of his children converted to Christianity. His grandson, Felix Mendelssohn the composer, was born a Christian.

When it was time for Moses Mendelssohn to marry, his father made arrangements for his warm and compassionate son to wed Fromet Guggenheim, a rich, young, and beautiful woman. They had never met. What made this union extraordinary was not only the humble origins of Mendelssohn, but his physical appearance. Though he had a brilliant mind, he was small, ugly, and a hunchback.

A party was arranged for the two to meet. While he was deeply engrossed in conversation, she had an opportunity to observe him from a distance, and was immediately repulsed. She emphatically informed her father that the engagement was off.

When Moses was informed that the woman did not wish to marry him, he requested and was granted a conversation with her alone. They talked quietly for a few moments before Mendelssohn said, "I wish to tell you a story."

"As you know," he began, "all marriages are arranged in heaven. Before I was born an angel was escorting me to earth. I asked if it was possible for me to see the woman God had selected for me. The angel answered that though it was highly unusual, he did not think it was impossible.

"I was granted one look, and to my astonishment the woman had an ugly hump on her back. I pleaded with God, 'It is not fair that a woman be a hunchback. She will be the object of scorn and contempt. I beg you, give me the hump and let her be well formed and beautiful.' "

Mendelssohn was silent a moment before he concluded. "God heard my prayer, and granted my wish. I am that boy and you are that girl."

Fromet Guggenheim looked at Moses Mendelssohn and viewed him with different eyes. The man she now saw and later married was wonderfully attractive, a man of warmth and compassion.

The Magic Ring

This story is adapted from a tale attributed to Moses Mendelssohn.

A woman once asked the Teacher, "Which is the true religion?" The Teacher replied: "Once there was a magic ring which gave its bearer the gifts of grace, kindness, and generosity. When the owner of the ring was on his deathbed, each of his three sons came separately and asked him for the ring. The old man promised the ring to each of them.

"He then sent for the finest jeweler in the land, and paid him to make two rings identical to the original. The jeweler did so, and before he died, the father gave each son a ring without telling him about the other two.

"Inevitably, the three sons discovered that each one had a ring, and they appeared before the local judge to ask his help in deciding who had the magic ring. The judge examined the rings and found them to be all alike. He then said, 'Why must anyone decide now? We shall know who has the magic ring when we observe the direction your life takes.'

"Each of the brothers then acted as if he had the magic ring by being kind, honest, and thoughtful.

"Now," the Teacher concluded, "religions are like the three brothers in the story. The moment their members cease striving for justice and love we will know that their religion is not the one God gave the world."

Compassion

The source of this story is a monastic community known as the Desert Fathers.

Three old men, one of whom had a bad reputation, came to visit the Teacher. The first one asked him, "Father, make me a fishing net."

"I will not make you one," he replied.

Then the second old man said, "Of your charity make me one, so that we have a souvenir of you in the monastery." But the Teacher said, "I do not have time."

Then the third one, who had a bad reputation, said, "Make me a fishing net, so that I may have something from your hand."

The Teacher answered at once, "For you, I will make one."

Later the two other old men asked him privately, "Why did you not want to do what we asked you, but you promised to do what he asked?"

The Teacher gave them this answer, "I told you I would not make one, and you were not disappointed, since you thought that

I had no time. But if I had not made one for him, he would have said, 'The Teacher has heard about my sin, and that is why he does not want to make me anything,' and so our relationship would have broken down. But now I have cheered his soul, so that he will not be overcome with grief. At times we must make special rules for our weaker friends."

A Most Precious Possession

A young convert approached a pastor with a question. "How can the holy God forgive a sinner? Isn't God repulsed with all of the hatred and jealousy that fills people?"

The pastor looked warmly at his young, enthusiastic friend and said, "You are the third generation in a family of master furniture makers. Tell me, if a fine table that your grandfather made was scratched would you throw it away?"

"Of course not," the young man exclaimed. "A scratch can hardly alter the character of a fine piece of furniture."

"And," the pastor continued, "if you nicked a well-crafted oak rocker would you toss it away?"

"Throw it away?" the young man exclaimed. "Even with a few scratches quality furniture is sturdy and valuable."

"You have spoken like a true craftsman," the pastor replied. "You share that spirit with our creator God who continues to find his human creation precious and valuable in spite of their obvious flaws."

Caught in the Act

Those who first read "Caught In the Act," unaware of the source of the story, commented that it is an unlikely story in today's world. Unfortunately they are correct. We have become so accustomed to sin that it no longer causes us alarm. We may not even call it sin. Yet this is based on events that occurred only a few years ago. The woman in this story was lucky enough to have a pastor who knew both the power of sin and the power of grace. He knew that unless we confess our sin we cannot be restored to full life in the community.

In a small midwestern town a woman was caught in the act of adultery. Her pastor visited her and found her brash and un-repentant. When he asked her to repent of her sin she cursed him and told him to leave. A few days later he brought two members of the church council to visit her. She laughed at all of them saying, "What I did was no big deal."

Finally, using Matthew 18:15-18, her case was brought before the members of her congregation who listened to the testimony and weighed it carefully. When everyone had spoken, one of the elders advised, "It is the recommendation of the council that we remove her from our group. We will continue to pray that she repents of her sin and that she will return to full fellowship." The congregation concurred.

In the days that followed her removal, the woman confronted several members of the church on the street and showered them with curses. Many women crossed the street in order to avoid her anger.

During the next few years the pastor frequently saw the woman and spoke to her. She never returned his greeting. Then one day they met quite by accident in a back aisle of the town's largest grocery story. "There is seldom a day that passes when I do not pray for you," the pastor said. The woman began to weep.

Two weeks later, on a Monday morning, the woman entered his study. No longer brassy and bold, she confessed her sin and asked for his guidance. In the weeks ahead the two met frequently for counseling and prayer. Then, one day, she asked, "What must I do to enter into the fellowship of the church again?"

He told her he would bring the issue before the meeting of

the whole church. When the congregation gathered the pastor told the people the story. When he finished, nearly a dozen people stood and recounted the tales of their encounters with the woman. The pastor reminded the people that those clashes took place prior to her confession.

Finally, the vote to reclaim her as a member took place. It lost by a substantial margin.

The pastor's face turned ashen when he heard the results. Before the president could adjourn the meeting, the pastor, trembling, stood and addressed the congregation. "Our Lord Jesus tells us that if our sister sins against us 70 times and asks for repentance, we must forgive her. You have chosen to ignore the command of Christ. I have no other choice than to declare that all of you who voted against her reinstatement are hereby placed under church discipline. Until you confess your sin you will not be allowed to eat at the Lord's table. Until this congregation repents, there shall be no absolution. I expect that those who voted for reinstatement will identify themselves."

At the next meeting of the congregation, the woman was restored to membership, by a unanimous vote.

5

STORIES OF PRAYER AND WORSHIP

Work and Prayer

"Be joyful always, pray continually."   1 Thessalonians 5:16-17

Several young men approached the Teacher and asked if they could join the community. The Teacher greeted them and assured them that they were welcome to stay as long as they desired. Then he added, "What kind of work do you do?"

"We do no manual labor," the spokesman replied. "We have devoted our entire life to prayer. If we are to become like the great prophets and saints of old we must pray without ceasing. Work stands in the path of prayer."

"Do you eat?" the Teacher asked the group.

"Certainly," came the puzzled reply.

"Do you sleep?"

"Of course," they answered with a trace of irritation.

The Teacher thought for a moment before he spoke again, "When you sleep and eat who prays for you?"

The young men were speechless.

The Teacher said, "Forgive me, but you make no sense. Contrary to your opinion, I find work an aid to prayer. As I work in the fields I pray without interruption. When I harvest the grain I repeat, 'Lord, have mercy on me, Christ have mercy on me, Lord have mercy on me.' When I do other menial tasks I rehearse the promises. Now I ask you, is this not prayer?"

With one voice they all agreed that the Teacher could both work and pray at the same time.

"Finally," he said, "I share half of all that I make with the poor. While I eat and sleep, those who received a portion of the fruit of my labor pray for me. Thus, by the grace of God as I work, I pray without ceasing."

Two Commandments

This story has little impact in a society that sees no value in fasting and has little fear of breaking commandments. In a different time, it was a powerful story. Perhaps it will be again.

Some visitors came a long distance to visit the Teacher during Holy Week. It was the custom of the entire community to fast the six days before Easter. As a way of showing his hospitality, the Teacher prepared a modest meal for his visitors. When some of the younger members of the fasting community saw the smoke from his chimney they approached the elders and said, "The Teacher has broken the rule and is cooking food at his place. You must speak with him."

One of the elders smiled and spoke for the rest. "Dear friends, the Teacher did indeed break the commandment that was established by the community, but in showing hospitality to strangers, he has firmly kept the commandment of God."

Free from Work

This story is based on a tale that comes from the Desert Fathers.

Young John approached the leader of the community. "I want to be free from work to worship God without interruption." Saying this, he took off his robe and went into the desert. After staying one week, he returned to the community. When he knocked on the Teacher's door the monk asked without opening it, "Who is it?"

"It is John, your friend."

The Teacher said, "My friend John has become an angel. He is not among our people anymore."

"No," John insisted, "it really is me."

But the Teacher did not open the door until the next morning. When the sun was about to rise, the Teacher came out of the house: "If you are a human being, you have to work again in order to live."

Then John repented, saying: "Forgive me, Teacher, for I was wrong."

The Shrine

Nasrudin's father was a highly respected keeper of a shrine, the burial place for a great teacher. Pilgrims traveled from long distances to pray at the holy place.

When he was fifteen Nasrudin bid his father farewell and left home with his donkey in pursuit of knowledge. He visited Egypt and Babylon before he set out for Tibet. While struggling across a mountain range in Kashmir his donkey died. Nasrudin mourned the loss of his faithful companion. He buried his old friend, built a mound of rocks over the grave and remained there in silent meditation.

As people made their way through the mountains they observed the solitary figure praying. "This must be the grave of a holy man, if his disciple mourns him," travelers concluded.

One day a rich man left money to build a shrine on that spot. Other pilgrims stopped to plant crops whose produce went to the upkeep of the shrine. The fame of the holy place spread until Nasrudin's father heard of it. He immediately set off to visit the sacred place. When his son told him the story of the death of his donkey the old man exclaimed, "The shrine where you were raised was developed under identical circumstances after the death of my own donkey, thirty years ago."

The Value of Knowledge

How much better to get wisdom than gold, to choose understanding rather than silver.   Proverbs 16:16

A distinguished scholar traveled on a boat with a large group of merchants. In the course of their conversation one of the merchants asked the scholar, "Good friend, what is your business?"

"I suppose you could say my business is knowledge and ideas. They are invaluable."

Several of the merchants ridiculed the scholar, "How do you sell an idea?" one cried. "I suppose he trades thoughts for bread and wine," another laughed.

Partway through the journey pirates overtook the ship, seized the entire cargo and stripped the passengers of their jewelry and fine clothes. Only the scholar, who carried no valuables and who was dressed modestly, was spared by the pirates.

When they landed, the scholar began to lecture on various subjects. The lectures created great interest and attracted large audiences from neighboring towns. Soon the scholar made friends and settled into the community.

On the other hand, the merchants, now dressed in rags, were unable to find employment. Finally, in desperation, they called upon the scholar and asked him to use his influence on their behalf. This he did, finding jobs for them all, proving that knowledge and ideas are indeed invaluable goods.

Full to the Top

This Japanese story seems especially appropriate for the season of Lent, a period when Christians are urged to let the self decrease and to allow Christ to increase.

A soldier approached the Teacher. "I have mastered all of the martial arts," he said calmly. "I have risen to the highest rank possible for a man of my training. I now wish to learn about God. Can you help me?"

The Teacher smiled and invited the man to sit at the table. "Let us have a cup of tea," he said, "before we talk further."

After the soldier sat, the Teacher began to pour tea into the man's cup. He filled the cup and kept on pouring until the tea was running over the table onto the floor. The soldier watched dumbfounded until he could no longer be silent. "Stop! It is full! The cup will not hold more tea!"

Placing the teapot on the table, the Teacher addressed the soldier, "You are so full of yourself that there is no room for God. It is not possible for you to learn until you empty yourself."

The Mad Dancers

"Why was it that so few understood Jesus?" the student asked the Teacher. "The Pharisees and scribes constantly opposed him. His disciples often seemed confused by his teaching, and still others suggested that he was possessed with demons. Even his own family feared for his mental health."

The Teacher replied, "Once there was a wedding couple who brought in the finest fiddlers and banjo players to entertain their guests immediately after the ceremony. The music was so captivating that soon everyone, young and old alike, began to dance. The people flung their bodies first one way and then another. The church was filled with joy.

"Two men drove by the church building in their new luxury automobile with the windows of the sedan rolled up and loud music blaring from their car radio. They could not hear a single sound from outside the automobile. When they saw people jumping around they stopped the car, shaking their heads at the sight. 'What a bunch of wierdos,' the driver said to his companion. 'See how they fling themselves about. I tell you the folks that go to that church are crazy.' "

The Teacher paused after finishing his story. "That is the conclusion people draw when they cannot hear the music to which others are dancing."

Three Sabbaths

The word sabbath *means "rest." (God blessed the seventh day and made it holy, because on it he rested—Genesis 2:2.) In the confrontations between Jesus and the Pharisees over Sabbath observance our Lord asked, "Which is lawful on the Sabbath: to do good or to do evil, to save life or to kill?" This story addresses that question.*

In a small village, three friends—a Moslem, a Jew, and a Christian—farmed on adjoining land. The Moslem observed Friday as the Sabbath, the Jew observed Saturday, and the Christian Sunday.

One autumn Friday around noon, the Jew and the Christian

finished plowing their fields. As he sat eating his lunch, the Christian noticed that the field of his Moslem friend was not yet plowed. "If he does not plow it today, it may rain tomorrow and he will not be able to complete his planting. I could plow a bit of his field and thus make his work easier." And he did.

In an adjoining field his Jewish companion came upon an identical plan. Without consulting with each other, the two men completed their neighbor's plowing.

The next day when the Moslem discovered that his field had been plowed, he rejoiced saying, "Surely God has sent his angels to plow my field while I observed his day of rest."

Months later, when harvest season arrived, the fields of the three friends flourished. One Sunday, the Jew and the Moslem were harvesting their crop while their Christian brother celebrated the Sabbath. As he completed harvesting his corn, the Jew noticed that the field of his Christian friend was ready to harvest. "If he does not harvest today, he could lose a part of his crop," he thought. "I will pick his corn until it becomes dark." And he did.

Completely unknown to him, his Moslem brother came to the same conclusion. Between them they harvested their friend's entire field.

On Monday, when the Christian came out to the field he discovered that his entire crop had been harvested. "It is a miracle," he thought. "While I rested, God's angels harvested."

During threshing season the Moslem and the Christian were working on a Saturday while their Jewish friend stayed at home, keeping the Sabbath holy. As he finished threshing his grain the Moslem looked to the next field and thought, "If my Jewish neighbor does not gather his grain today the rain might wash it away and he will lose his crop. I will thresh part of his crop this afternoon." And he did.

Unknown to him, his Christian friend decided upon the same

course of action. Separately, the two men threshed, bound, and covered the entire crop.

When his sabbath was over, the Jewish farmer discovered that his grain was threshed. Lifting his eyes to heaven he prayed, "Blessed are you, Lord God of the universe, for sending your angels while I was keeping your Sabbath."

In the Presence

Prayer is more than speaking and words. Ultimately it is being in the presence of God.

Three monks made their annual trip to visit a wise and holy man. Two of the brothers asked many questions and shared thoughts and dreams, but the third companion remained silent and spoke not a word. After many visits the Teacher spoke to the silent brother. "Though you come here often, you ask me no questions." Smiling, the brother replied, "It is enough just to be with you, father."

6

STORIES OF COMMUNITY AND HOSPITALITY

A Party for Coats

This delightful story is adapted from a Turkish folktale.

"You must hurry," friends cried to the Teacher as he rushed home from the fields. "The banquet at the home of Halil has already begun. You are late."

They are right, the Teacher thought. *If I take the time to change clothes, I could miss the entire dinner.* Instead of returning to his home he proceeded in his work clothes to the home of Halil, the rich man.

When he arrived the servants at the door refused to allow him to enter because he was not dressed properly. Though he protested, the servants stood firm.

Finally, the Teacher walked to the home of a friend who lived nearby. He borrowed a nice coat and quickly returned to the party. He was immediately welcomed and was seated at the banquet table.

When the food was served, the Teacher began to put it on his coat. He smeared his jacket with vegetables and poured the appetizer in his pocket. All the time he said loudly, "Eat, dear dinner jacket. I hope you are enjoying the meal."

All the guests focused their attention on the Teacher's strange behavior. Finally, Halil asked, "Why are you telling your jacket to enjoy the meal?"

"When I arrived in my work clothes," the Teacher explained, "I was refused entrance. It was only when I was accompanied by this fine coat that I was allowed to sit at the table. Naturally I assume that it was the jacket, not me, that was invited to your banquet."

Imitating Rebekah

This story is based on Genesis 24:10-27, the encounter between Rebekah and the servant of Abraham.

The Teacher, traveling on a hot summer day, began to look for a cool drink of water. Late in the afternoon he came to a small village where a young lady was drawing water from a well. "May I have a drink from your bucket?" the Teacher asked.

Immediately the girl handed the bucket filled with cool water to the Teacher saying, "Drink as much as you like. When you are finished I will also draw water for your animal." The Teacher smiled at the young woman and said, "Your kindness imitates Rebecca at the well."

"Perhaps you in turn will imitate faithful Eliezer," the woman replied.

"If I had a gold ring and two gold bracelets I would gladly give them to you," the Teacher said. "But it is obvious that you possess something much more valuable than gold jewelry, a generous and hospitable spirit. Instead of gifts I offer you my thanks and my prayers that God will assist you in retaining your charitable spirit throughout your life."

Only One Father

A student approached the Teacher with excitement. "I have just discovered a mistake in the Gospel of Mark," he announced proudly. "In Mark 10:29 Jesus answered Peter by saying, 'I tell you the truth, no one who was left home or brothers or sisters or mother or father or children or fields for me and the gospel will fail to receive a hundred times as much in this present age (homes, brothers, sisters, mothers, children and fields—and with them, persecutions) and in the age to come, eternal life.' "

"And the mistake?" asked the Teacher.

"Even you don't see it?" the student said triumphantly. "Though he mentions fathers in the first part, he does not promise people a hundredfold of fathers."

"Ah," the Teacher said, "the omission was deliberate. Our Lord was teaching us that whoever entered into Christian community would increase the number of their family many times. They would no longer have a few brothers or sisters. They would no longer have one mother. They would have many new Christian brothers and sisters and mothers. But as for fathers, there is need of only one, our Father in heaven. Remember, Jesus did teach us to call no one father save our Creator God."

Hospitality

Folktales often use hyperbole to make a point. In this story the radical act of the host tells how important the act of hospitality is in the Near Eastern world.

In a country that honored hospitality and fine horses above everything else, there once was a man who owned the most beautiful thoroughbred stallion of all. It was coveted by all his neighbors. Seldom did a day pass when he was not made a generous offer for the high-spirited animal. No matter what price he was offered he refused.

Among those who desired the animal was his friend, a horse-dealer. Though the dealer made many generous offers they were always politely refused.

One day, hearing that the horse's owner had fallen on hard times, the dealer decided to visit. "If I make a generous offer now," he thought, "I will gain the horse and my friend's fortune will be restored."

As was the custom in that country, the two men ate before any business was transacted. A meal was presented and the two men ate their full.

Finally, it came time for the horse dealer to make his offer. The owner listened carefully before he replied, "It is no longer possible for me to sell you the horse. Since I had nothing else to serve, we had to kill the horse, thus discharging my obligation as host."

Though he was deeply disappointed, the horse-dealer understood. Hospitality was more important than business.

Stone Soup

This old American folktale not only shows us the advantage of being clever, but the beauty of community and sharing—values assumed and urged by Jesus and the New Testament writers. Children love this story and enjoy helping the storyteller prepare the soup by bringing wood, water, and imaginary vegetables to an imaginary pot.

A soldier rode his tired horse down a back country road on his way home from an ill-advised battle. In truth, to this soldier all battles seemed ill-advised, for he saw little sense to violence or killing.

It was late afternoon and the man was tired and hungry. Up ahead he saw a small village. "I'll get something to eat there and find a place for the night," he thought.

Suddenly the horse tripped, throwing the soldier to the ground. As he brushed himself off, he saw that the horse had stumbled over a rock sticking out of the ground in the middle of the road. He walked back to the rock, and with the help of his sword, dug it out of the earth. It was a splendid rock, almost perfectly round and smooth. The soldier liked the rock, so rather than throw it away he put it in his saddle bags, climbed upon his horse, and continued into the village.

As he rode past the first houses the village people stopped their work to stare. He waved to several of the townsfolk, but no one waved back. Dismounting, the soldier approached a woman standing in front of a small house. "Good evening," he said cheerfully. "Could you spare a bit of food for a hungry man?"

The woman shook her head sadly and sighed, "We have had a poor harvest. There is barely enough for our family. I am sorry." With these words she walked into the house.

The man continued to the next house where a farmer was working on his wagon. "Do you have a place at your table for a hungry soldier?" he asked.

"It didn't rain during the last month before harvest," the farmer said. "What little we have is needed for our children."

At every home he visited, the soldier heard the same sad story: The harvest had been poor, there was not enough food to make it through the winter, the family needed the grain for seed.

Completely discouraged, and very hungry, the soldier tied his horse to the branch of a tree and sat down. "In a few weeks these poor people will be as hungry as I am," he thought. "I wish I could help them find food."

Suddenly an idea hit him. He reached into his saddle bags,

took out the stone and addressed the villagers. "Ladies and gentle-men," the soldier shouted, "you are fortunate that I came to your town. I have in my hands a special rock that will help take you through the long winter. This is a magic rock. With it you can make stone soup."

"Stone soup?" an old man repeated. "I have never heard of stone soup."

"The wonder of stone soup," the soldier continued, "is that it not only feeds hungry people, it helps bring people together. Now, who has a large empty iron kettle?"

Quickly a huge iron pot was found, and delivered to the soldier in a wheel barrow. "The kettle is barely large enough, but it will do," the soldier said. "Now we must fill the pot with water and start a fire."

Eager hands carried buckets of water and firewood. Soon the pot was placed over a roaring fire. As the water began to boil the soldier dramatically raised the magic stone above his head, and then he gently placed it in the kettle.

"The stone looks just like the ones we have in our backyard," a little boy whispered to his mother.

The mother picked up the child and assured him, "You can't tell if something is magic by looking at the outside."

"Stone soup needs salt and pepper," the soldier announced.

Two children ran to find salt and pepper.

After the water had boiled for a few minutes the soldier sipped the brew. "This stone makes excellent soup, but it would be better if we had a few carrots."

"I have a few carrots that I'm willing to share," a farmer replied. Immediately his daughter ran home and returned with an apron full of carrots.

"It is too bad the harvest was so bad," the soldier said sadly. "Stone soup is always more tasty when we add a cabbage or two."

"I think I know where to find a cabbage," a young mother

shouted over her shoulder as she left for home. When she returned she was carrying three large cabbages.

The soldier was busy slicing carrots and cabbages with his sword. "The last time I made stone soup was at the castle of a rich man. He added a few potatoes and bit of beef."

Several people talked quietly. "A bit of beef and we can eat like rich people," they whispered. They went home and soon returned not only with beef and potatoes but milk, onions, and barley.

By the time the soup was ready it was almost dark. Men brought large tables, women brought soup bowls and others carried cider and bread. It was the most delicious soup they had ever smelled, and to think it all came from the magic stone.

After everyone ate their fill people brought out the fiddles. They danced and sang until the wee hours of the night. Never had people experienced such a wonderful party.

The next morning the whole village gathered to say good-bye to the soldier. As he mounted his horse a small child cried, "You are forgetting the magic stone."

"I am leaving the stone with you as a gift," the soldier smiled.

As the soldier rode off a young girl said to her grandfather, "As long as we have the magic stone we shall never be hungry."

"Remember," the grandfather added, "that the soldier promised another bit of magic from the stone. He said that the stone also brings people closer together."

They both agreed that the stone had done everything the soldier had promised.

St. Jerome and the Lion

This legend demonstrates two themes often found in folk literature. The first theme is the interdependence of animals and humans. These tales, which are legion, draw a picture of the peaceable kingdom, where

the lion not only lies down with the lamb, but also with human friends.
A second theme might be called virtue repaid. In this story the lion repays
Jerome's kindness with his deep loyalty.

In the fifth century Jerome and a small group of monks lived
in a monastery at Bethlehem. One day as the monks left the
chapel after vespers, a lion limped into the monastery courtyard.
All the monks fled in fear. Some jumped through windows and
others hid in the attic. Only Jerome stood still. He watched with
interest as the wounded lion moved toward him slowly. Finally
the great beast stopped and lifted his paw.

Jerome approached the lion and examined the ailing limb.
Immediately he discovered a large splinter buried deep in the
flesh. Quickly, he took a pair of pliers and removed the wood.
Then he bathed the lion's paw, cleaned the wound and wrapped
it with a clean linen.

Instead of leaving the courtyard, as the monks hoped and ex-
pected, the animal curled up near Jerome's cell and fell asleep.
As the days passed the lion began to act like a permanent guest.
Jerome was not pleased.

One day when the old monk was convinced that the lion's paw
was healed he asked all the monks to gather in the courtyard
around the animal. "No one can remain at this monastery and
remain idle. Everyone must have a job, including you," Jerome
said to the lion. "Your task will be to accompany the donkey
who goes into the forest for firewood each day. You will provide
protection from robbers and wolves." The lion waved its giant
tail as if he understood.

Most of the other monks thought Jerome's idea was crazy. They
could imagine the lion eating the donkey, not protecting him.
But in the days ahead the plan seemed to work perfectly.

Each morning the donkey, accompanied by an old man, went
into the forest. The lion went along and kept watch. When they
gathered enough wood, the three returned home.

One hot afternoon, when the lion was keeping watch, he fell asleep. While he slept, traveling merchants bound the old man and took both the man and the donkey.

When he awoke the lion searched everywhere for his beloved friends without success. At last he returned to the monastery where he was met by an irate group of monks. "We knew he'd do it," they cried. "He has killed the man and eaten the donkey." Even Jerome's confidence was shaken. The old monk declared that the lion should take the donkey's place. A harness was made for the king of the beasts who was driven into the forest each day to fetch wood.

One afternoon the lion saw a caravan of merchants passing in the distance with his friend the donkey leading their camels. The lion leaped forward, upsetting the man who was loading him and scattering the wood everywhere. He raced toward the donkey who greeted him with great joy. The terrified merchants, running for their lives, went straight to the monastery for sanctuary, and there confessed their sins. "The old man is safe in Damascus," they cried. "Forgive us and spare our lives."

First, Jerome forgave the merchants. Then he and the other monks publicly confessed their sin against the gentle beast, who seemed content just to have his old friend back.

If you ever see a picture of St. Jerome, you will see a lion lying contentedly at his feet.

A Blessing or a Curse?

According to Italian legend, there was a day when Jesus traveled through Europe and Africa with his disciples. The stories that recount these legends are earthy and humorous. At the same time they also teach.

One evening about sundown Jesus was walking with St. Peter when they stopped at the home of a wealthy couple. "Do you

have a place where two travelers can lay their weary bones?" asked
the Lord.

"Do I look like an innkeeper?" shouted an irate woman as she
slammed the door.

Without a word Jesus walked across the road to a very modest
home. He knocked on the door and a woman carrying a small
baby answered. "Would you be so kind as to give us a night's
lodging?" Jesus asked.

"It is an honor to share our home with you," the woman said
enthusiastically. "Surely you are hungry. Go warm yourselves by
the fire and I'll get you something as soon as I put the children
to bed."

As they stepped inside the Lord and Peter saw three youngsters
peeking out of a small bedroom. The woman excused herself and
disappeared inside the bedroom. The two men could hear the
voices of the children saying their prayers. Soon the woman rushed
out of the room and quickly prepared sandwiches for the travelers.

When Jesus and Peter awoke the next morning they found a
wonderful breakfast sitting on the table. "I trust that you slept
well last night," the woman said.

As the men ate the woman prepared school lunches for the
children and put soup on the fire for the evening meal. When
they got ready to leave she handed Jesus a small bag. "It isn't
much, but it is will be better than what you can get at some
greasy inn."

The Lord was clearly impressed with the treatment they had
received. "We'd like to thank you for your hospitality. I'm the
Lord Jesus, and this is Peter. Whatever you start out doing this
morning you will continue to do all through the day." Then they
waved good-bye and left.

As soon as the children left for school the woman started weaving. Never had things gone so well or had she weaved so fine.
By the time the children returned from school she had weaved
enough cloth to fill a whole room. After the evening meal she

wove again. Just before she was ready to quit her neighbor from across the road stopped by and was startled to see all the cloth. The woman told her the whole story.

"Had I known it was the Lord I would have found room for them at my house," the woman said. "Do you expect them again?"

"They said they would be back in a week or so."

"Please, be so kind as to send them to my house so they can bless me."

"I will be happy to do so."

In a few days the Lord and Peter stopped by the home of their friend about the same time. The woman explained that her neighbor had more room and would be honored if the two men would spend the night at her house.

"She doesn't want us," muttered Peter as they crossed the street. "All she wants is the blessing."

"Some people can turn a blessing into a curse," the Lord observed as he knocked on the door.

This time the Lord and Peter were treated with great kindness. The kitchen was filled with freshly baked foods. As the woman ran back and forth to the table she barked out orders to her husband. "Pick up the kettle! Get more wood! Watch where you are going."

The Lord and Peter slept in the guest room and rose in the morning to a fine breakfast. As they prepared to eat the Lord said, "Whatever you begin doing this morning you shall continue throughout the day."

As soon as the two men were out of sight the husband set up the loom so that his wife could begin weaving. "I will weave twice as much cloth as my neighbor," the woman exclaimed.

Before she settled down to weaving, so she wouldn't be interrupted, the woman decided to go to the outhouse to relieve herself. Once she began she found that she couldn't stop. Several times she tried to get to the loom, but as soon as she sat down she had to run outside again. She spent the entire day there until it was time to go to bed.

Abraham's Hospitality

One source credits this story to the Talmud. Another Jewish source says that the writer of this story was Ben Franklin.

The tent of Abraham and Sarah was constantly open to strangers for they both knew that hospitality was a gift that came directly from God.

One day Abraham invited an old man to join him for a meal. When they finished eating the old man thanked his host for their fine gift. "You need not thank me," Abraham assured him. "Whatever I have given you comes from the God of creation. Thank God."

"Why would I bother to thank your God when I have my own?" the old man said reaching into his pack. He drew out a wooden idol and set it on the floor. "This is the god who I intend to thank for taking care of me."

Abraham was furious. "How dare you worship a god made with hands," he shouted. He seized the man and threw him out of the tent. "I am sorry that I ever wasted my hospitality on you," he concluded.

Before the old man was out of sight Abraham heard a voice calling his name.

"Yes, Lord?" the patriarch answered.

"For 80 years I have protected and cared for the old man you just threw out of your tent. All this time, though he has given credit to his wooden idol, I have continued to claim him as my own. Although he knows no better, Abraham, you do. Now go, find the old man, and bring him back. Make him welcome. You are to serve even those who do not understand that there is but one God."

And Abraham once again obeyed God.

The Bundle of Sticks

This story is based on a fable of Aesop.

There was once a father who had five sons who were constantly quarreling. One day, weary from their bickering, he asked them to bring him a bundle of sticks. Handing the bundle to the oldest he commanded, "Break it." The lad attempted to break the sticks over his knee, but his reward was a sore leg. One by one the other brothers were given the same command. None of them were able to break the bundle.

Finally, the father tore open the bundle and handed each son a single stick. "Break it," he said. The task was done with little effort.

"My sons, if you remain together and assist one another you will have the strength of this bundle. If, however, you are divided among yourselves you will be broken as easily as these sticks."

The Ass and the Mule

This is another fable attributed to Aesop.

A man set forth on a journey with his ass and a mule both carrying a heavy load. As he traveled along the plain, the ass carried his load with ease, but when he began to climb the mountain, his load was more than he could bear. "I beg you," the ass whispered to the mule, "relieve me by accepting a small portion of my load."

The mule shook his head, "Each of us has been assigned a task. You carry your load and I will carry mine."

Shortly after their conversation, the ass fell to the ground dead. The man took the load carried by the ass and placed it on the mule. In addition, he skinned the ass and added the hide to the load carried by the mule.

Groaning under his heavy load, the mule said to himself, "If I had only been willing to assist the ass a little, I would not have to bear his entire burden."

7

STORIES OF JUSTICE AND COURAGE

The High Price of Punishment

This story is adapted from a tale by Leo Tolstoy who, in turn, adapted a work of Guy de Maupassant.

On the shores of the Mediterranean Sea, between France and Italy, lies the tiny kingdom of Monaco. Our story takes place many years ago when the population numbered only 7,000 people. In those days the King of Monaco had a difficult time finding money to meet expenses. Even though he imposed taxes, there were few people to pay them. In desperation, he turned to gambling to increase revenue. Though gambling brought in people from other countries, and though it increased the amount of money the king had to run the country, the kingdom remained poor and the people thrifty.

One day, around the turn of the last century, there was a murder in this tiny kingdom. People were astonished for nothing like this had ever happened before. Judges who had never presided over a murder trial scrambled to understand the correct legal procedures. Finally, everything was set. After a lengthy trial a jury found a man guilty and sentenced him to having his head cut off.

"Splendid decision," the king declared. "However, there does seem to be a problem. We have no guillotine, and no executioner."

"It is my considered opinion," intoned the Minister of Justice, "that our problem can be solved by writing the French government and requesting to borrow a machine and an executioner."

"Splendid idea!" cried the king. That day a letter was sent by courier to the French government.

Quickly the courier returned with an answer from the king of France, which the Minister of Justice read aloud. "France will be happy to send us a guillotine and an expert to use it for the sum of sixteen thousand francs."

"Sixteen thousand francs!" the king stormed. "The wretch isn't worth it. Surely there must be a cheaper way to cut off his head."

"We could write the king of Italy to see if he would rent his machine for less," offered another of the king's advisors.

"Splendid idea!" the king shouted. "Send a letter immediately."

The reply from the Italian government arrived in less than a week. "We would be honored to send our finest machine and an expert to teach you how to use it for only twelve thousand francs," the letter read.

"The scoundrel isn't worth twelve thousand francs," the king thundered. "Why, that would be almost two francs for every inhabitant in the land. Think!" he shouted, "Think of a cheaper solution."

"Your majesty," a timid minister said weakly, "we could engage our army in the execution. After all, the army is paid to kill people."

When the general of the army was brought before the king and told of the plan he protested, "No one in the army has killed a man in years. You know that we don't even issue bullets. The army is used for parades and state functions, nothing more. Even so, this man must have his head cut off. None of my men know how to use a sword."

In desperation the king appointed a committee to study the problem and make a recommendation. After several meetings they came back to the king with this advice. "Your majesty, we suggest that you commute the sentence from death to life imprisonment. You will show mercy on the man and it will save you the cost of the execution."

"Splendid idea!" shouted the king. "There is only one problem. We don't have a prison, or a guard for the prison." After some effort a small room was discovered on the palace grounds not far from the palace kitchen. A guard was hired to stand at the door to bring the criminal's food from the kitchen.

At the end of a year the royal treasurer approached the king. "Your majesty, I have just finished calculating the cost of imprisoning our criminal for the past year. This figure naturally includes everything including the guard's salary. Your majesty, the total cost for one year is six hundred francs!"

"Six hundred francs!" the king shouted. "This is an outrage. The scoundrel is young and healthy. He could live for another fifty years!"

The king called his royal advisors and demanded, "You must find a cheaper method of dealing with this miserable lout. He is costing us too much money."

After a long period of silence, the Minister of Justice said, "I suggest that we dismiss the guard. After all, his salary is the major part of the six hundred francs."

"Without a guard the man will escape," a second advisor reminded the group.

"Correct," the minister said with a big smile. "We let him escape so we won't have to feed or house him any more."

"Splendid idea!" the king shouted. He immediately dismissed the guard.

Now all of the king's advisors hid in a building across the street to watch the escape. The criminal, however, didn't move until it was time to eat. At noon he walked outside to look for the guard. When he did not find him he went to the palace kitchen to get his dinner. He took what was given him, returned to prison, and closed the door. He stayed in his quarters until the next meal when he repeated the same process. This continued for two days.

The king's advisors went into emergency session to solve the latest problem with the criminal. This time they appointed the Minister of Justice to tell the man that he was free to leave.

"You no longer have a guard," the Minister of Justice said to the prisoner. "The king will not be offended if you leave immediately."

"I don't care what does or doesn't offend the king," the prisoner replied. "I have nowhere to go. You have ruined my reputation with your sentence. No one will hire me. Besides, it is about time that this country learns to keep its word. First you tell me you are going to kill me and you don't. Next you say that you will imprison me for life, and you change your mind again. Now you take away my guard and make me get my own meals. I don't trust you. I'm not going anywhere!"

The king's advisors were thoroughly confused. How should they deal with the expensive prisoner? Finally after consulting the king the ministers made the prisoner an offer. "We will give you a yearly pension of four hundred francs," they said.

"No way," the prisoner countered. "I'm not moving for less than four hundred fifty. Plus, I want another 50 francs for the downpayment on a house."

After a quick consultation, the ministers agreed. The man

bought a small house, planted a vegetable garden and lived very well. Each year, on the same date, he took the train to the palace and picked up his check. He was a lucky man. He had a home and security. Most important, he was fortunate that he didn't commit his crime in a country where they did not begrudge the expense of cutting off a man's head or imprisoning him for life.

A Time to Cast Away

For everything there is a season, and a time for every matter under heaven: . . . a time to seek, and a time to lose; a time to keep, and a time to cast away.   Ecclesiastes 3:1,6 RSV

A merchant and his son were traveling over the sea, carrying a large sum of money with them, when they overheard some of the sailors planning to kill them and share in the spoil. Quickly the father and son planned a strategy. They pretended to quarrel on deck, and in the heat of the argument the father threw all the money overboard. Since there was no longer any reason to kill them, the sailors did them no harm.

When they arrived at their destination the merchant and his son swore out a warrant against their would-be assassins, who were immediately put in jail. Next they sued the owners of the vessel for the recovery of the money. The defendants argued that the money was voluntarily thrown into the sea, but the judge ruled in the merchant's favor saying, "The man was justified in throwing the money overboard to save both his own life and that of his son. For everything there is a season, and a time for every matter under heaven: a time to keep, and a time to cast away."

Fatting for the Kill

The following story is a Jewish folktale.

A young donkey brought a complaint to his father, "There is no justice on this farm. You and I work all day long pulling heavy loads for the master while that pig lays around in the sun. Yet the master feeds the pig more than he feeds us. Why, the pig is nice and fat while our ribs are showing."

"Do not judge things by appearance," answered the older animal. "The pig's life-style will ultimately be his undoing. When he gets a bit fatter the master will kill him."

The Will

This man will not be your heir, but a son coming from your own body will be your heir.   Genesis 15:4

A man who was blessed with wisdom, virtue, and wealth had only one son. He offered him the best education, sending him to Jerusalem to learn. He made certain the young man's every need was met.

Shortly after his son left, he became sick and died. His death caused immense grief throughout the community, for he was a benefactor for both rich and poor alike.

When the period of mourning was over, the dead man's executor opened the man's will and read it aloud. To the astonishment of everyone, the man left all of his property and wealth to his slave. There was a final clause that his beloved son should have the privilege of choosing only one thing out of the entire estate.

Immersed in grief over the loss of his father, the young man asked his teacher to assist him in selecting one thing from his father's estate. In the meantime, the slave began to live the life of a wealthy man.

When the teacher read the will, he at once discovered the intention of the father. "We must leave at once for your home," the teacher told his pupil, "where you will take possession of all your property."

"But I am a pauper," the boy cried. "All I have are the clothes on my back and one item from my father's house."

"I suggest," the teacher said, "that you choose your late father's slave out of his estate, and with him will go over to you all he possesses, since a slave can own nothing, and all he has belongs to his master. That indeed was your father's clever device. He knew that if the will were to state that all was left to you, the slave, in your absence, would take for himself all the valuables on which he could lay his hands. Whereas, if he thought all belonged to him, he would take care of everything that was left. Your father knew that the one thing he gave you the power to choose would be no other than his slave, and with him you will become the just and rightful owner of everything."

A Cup of Water

"The world rests on three things," the rabbis taught. "The study of Scripture, prayer, and loving-kindness." The word for "loving-kindness," gemilut hasadim, referred to the giving of self. This story, adapted from a Jewish folktale, tells of gemilut hasadim.

A famous rabbi and his friends had spent the entire morning working far from the village. The labor was difficult and dirty. At noon his friends brought a pail of water so their teacher could wash his hands thoroughly. To their surprise he used only a few drops. How could it be that this pious Jew would skimp on the commandment to wash completely before eating?

Cautiously, one of his friends said, "Rabbi, you used so little water. It was not nearly enough to get your hands clean."

Wordlessly, the rabbi pointed to a servant girl coming up the path from the well. She was bent low under a heavy bar laid across her shoulders. From the two ends of the bar hung massive pails of water.

"How could I do the washing at the expense of this poor girl?" the rabbi asked. "The water I save may prevent one trip to the well for her."

Later the friends talked about the rabbi's action. They learned that in certain circumstances obedience to the commandments comes at the expense of others. They also understood that loving-kindness is the greatest of all virtues.

The Burning of the Rice Fields

This wonderful story comes from Japan.

Long ago in Japan there was a small village. To the east of the village was the great ocean; to the west a high mountain. Some of the men made their living by fishing while all the other villagers—men, women, and children—worked in the rice fields that lay on top of the mountain. Each morning the villagers climbed the mountain path to work. Each evening they trudged home to sleep in their huts. Only grandfather, and his grandson, Ti, lived on the mountain, where it was grandfather's job to keep the fires lit at night to ward off the wild animals.

Early one morning, during the season when the rice fields had turned gold and dry, ready for the harvest, grandfather stirred the fire for the last time. Down below, the villagers began to move about doing their morning chores before they started their trek to the top of the mountain. When the fire roared again, grandfather went to the edge of the mountain to watch the sun rise. This morning, however, he could not see the rising sun. What he saw brought fear to his soul.

Quickly he ran to the hut where Ti was still sleeping. "Ti, get up."

"Oh, grandfather, let me sleep."

"Do as I say," the old man shouted. "Get a burning stick from the fire."

This time Ti obeyed, for he had never heard grandfather sound so urgent. Without understanding, Ti got up, took a burning stick from the fire, and then went out to join grandfather who was thrusting his burning stick into the dry rice. Grandfather spit out a command, "Burn the rice fields."

"But grandfather, this is our village's food. Without it we will all go hungry!"

"Do as I do," grandfather shouted over his shoulder.

With tears steaming down his face, Ti took the burning stick and began to set the precious rice fields on fire. Soon smoke from the rice fields billowed up, filling the sky.

Down below the villagers saw the smoke and the priests began to ring the bells to alert the people who were not outside. Soon every man, woman, and child ran up the steep mountain path as quickly as they could. When they finally reached the top all they could see were the flames consuming their precious rice. Everything was destroyed.

"Who set the fire?" the people cried.

Grandfather stepped forward and said, "I did it."

"You, grandfather? But why?"

"Look," grandfather said, pointing out to the sea. What they witnessed was a gigantic tidal wave rushing ominously toward shore. When it reached the village it crushed the houses like a giant hand smashing paper cups. Soon a second wave and a third followed, covering the village under tons of water. The villagers looked at their ruined homes and their burnt fields in despair.

"We have nothing left," one voice cried.

"On the contrary," an old woman countered. "We have our lives. Everyone has survived."

"This afternoon we will start all over," the village elder said. "But first, we must thank grandfather for his act of courage and wisdom. His action saved our people."

All of the people agreed. For the rest of his life the village honored grandfather for his courage and wisdom.

A Terrible Mercy

"A Terrible Mercy" is adapted from a Turkish story.

While a man slept, a poisonous creature crept in his mouth and got caught in his throat.

Suddenly he woke up and started to cough and shake in order to rid himself of the creature. No matter what he tried, it failed.

A man on horseback, who just happened by, immediately understood the man's dilemma.

For a moment he sat frozen, unable to think of a plan. Then, when an idea hit him, he began to beat the man violently. Using his whip, the horseman flailed away at the poor man until he begged for mercy. When a crowd gathered the man begged them to intercede for him, but an old woman prevented anyone from moving forward. Finally, with a mighty heave, the poisonous creature was thrown up by the protesting stomach of the afflicted man.

The creature fell to the ground and slithered away.

The horseman removed his cloak and covered the recovering man who lay shivering on the ground. The old woman brought water and bathed his forehead.

Finally the man was able to lift himself and speak, "Now that you have beaten me silly, you offer me comfort. What is with you?"

The old woman was quick to speak, "Don't you understand? The horseman's assault was the only way you could rid yourself of the creature before it injected venom into your system. By beating you he saved your life."

Two Pebbles

This story is based on a Jewish folktale.

When a boy was found dead, the authorities arrested a young man with a reputation as a troublemaker. This was an opportunity to solve the murder, and at the same time get rid of the man they considered the town nuisance.

After a long argument, the judge said, "I suggest we use the ancient tradition of drawing lots in order to determine the guilt of this man. I shall put two pebbles in this bowl. If he draws the white pebble we will know he is innocent. If he draws the black pebble, it will be clear that he is guilty."

The young man watched carefully as the judge picked two small stones off the ground, and placed them in the dark bowl. Although he couldn't see what was picked, he suspected that the judge had set a trap by placing two black pebbles in the bowl.

As the young man drew the pebble out of the bowl he dropped it on the ground, where it was immediately lost among all the other small stones. "You are not only cruel, you are clumsy," shouted the judge. "Now we will have to draw stones again."

"Not at all," cried the young man. Reaching in the bowl, he picked out a black stone. "If all that is left is the black stone, then surely the one I dropped was the white one. I am innocent."

And they let him go.

Ruth and Tobias

According to Hebrew legend Elijah, who was taken bodily into heaven, frequently returns to earth to assist the poor.

A long time ago, a poor scribe whose name was Tobias lived with his wife, Ruth, and their five children. Though Tobias worked long hours copying the sacred scrolls, there was never much money.

One day Tobias fell while carrying wood and injured his right hand. Now even his meager income ceased. Ruth was unable to buy food for the table or clothes for the children. When the family complained, Tobias reassured them, "God is good; God will provide."

Finally, Ruth said to him, "It is time to make yourself available for God's miracle. Go to the streets where God can find you."

"All I have is rags to wear," Tobias protested.

"I have borrowed a coat and a hat from the neighbors," his wife informed him. Quickly she helped her husband dress and then waved good-bye. "God be with you," she said gently.

As Tobias approached the center of the city an old man with a white beard stopped him. "Shalom, Tobias," the man said. "I have been waiting many days for you to come."

"I am afraid I do not know your name," Tobias said.

"My name is Elijah and I have a gift for you."

"What kind of a gift?" Tobias asked in astonishment.

"My gift to you is this: You and your family shall enjoy seven years of wealth, happiness, and comfort. All you need to do is to tell me whether you want these seven years now or at the close of your life."

Tobias said, "If this decision affects my entire family, I must consult them. May I give you my decision in the morning?"

"Certainly," the prophet replied. "I will meet you here to-morrow for your answer."

Tobias rushed home to tell his wife the entire story. When he finished she was quiet for a few moments before she spoke. "To-morrow you must tell Elijah to send us the good years now, for the present is to be preferred over what is far off."

When Elijah met Tobias the next day he asked for his decision. "Let the seven good years begin immediately," the scribe replied.

"It shall be as you ask," said Elijah. "By the time you reach home, the Lord will have granted you good fortune."

Tobias immediately set out for his home. When he arrived his

children showed him a treasure they found while digging in the
ground. The entire family gathered and Tobias gave thanks to
God for his great mercy. When he concluded his prayers, he said
to the children, "It was your mother who decided that we should
receive the gift now. It was sound advice."

The good woman smiled, "Since God will bless us for seven
years we will be good stewards of his gifts and share our good
fortune with the hungry and others in need." For seven years
Ruth and Tobias practiced charity toward people in need. No
one who appealed for help from them was denied. Ruth wrote
everything they dispensed to the poor in a book.

One day Elijah appeared to Ruth and Tobias as they were
walking down the road. "The time has come," the prophet said,
"for me to withdraw the gift I gave you."

"Please," Ruth said quietly, "walk with us to our home."
When they arrived at their modest home Ruth handed the book
of records to the prophet and said, "If you can find anyone more
faithful than my husband and me to care for the treasure then
we shall freely let it go."

God was pleased with the faithfulness of Ruth and Tobias, for
he saw that they had used the gifts given them for good. He
continued to bestow his mercy upon them and allowed them to
keep the wealth until the end of their lives.

Blood Money

"Blood Money" comes out of the rich tradition of Italian folklore.

Each morning Brother Martin, the youngest of the novices,
went out begging for the monastery. After several months he had
developed a daily route. From a few kind shopkeepers he received
a few coins. The baker always provided a few loaves of bread.
Most of the food Martin received came from poor people, who
gave cheerfully.

Though his daily route took him past the office of a lawyer named Grubbs, Martin never approached him. Grubbs was a man who made most of his living renting run-down homes to the poor. Townspeople knew him as the biggest slum landlord.

One day lawyer Grubbs, offended that Brother Martin passed him up, went to the monastery to complain to the prior. "I'm an important man in this community," Grubbs shouted. "Your novice treats me as if I am trash."

Not wishing to offend a wealthy man, the prior assured him that Brother Martin would visit him the next morning. When the lawyer left, the prior called the young novice. "It is not your task to judge the character of those who wish to contribute to the work of this monastery. Tomorrow I want you to take two sacks to the office of Mr. Grubbs and accept whatever he gives you."

Brother Martin silently agreed. The next morning his first stop was at the office of the lawyer. While Grubbs filled the two sacks, he told Brother Martin what an honest and God-fearing man he was. The novice never spoke a word.

When the lawyer finished loading the sacks, Brother Martin threw them over his shoulders and headed back to the monastery. He hadn't walked more than a step before a drop of blood fell from the sacks. The farther he walked, the more blood fell. People along the way who noticed the sacks dripping blood, said, "It looks like a meat day at the monastery. They will feast tonight!" Without a word, Brother Martin continued on his way, leaving a trail of blood behind him.

When he reached the monastery, the brothers who saw him come in with blood-stained sacks exclaimed, "Brother Martin is bringing meat today! And freshly slaughtered!" They opened the knapsacks, but they contained no meat. "Where did all the blood come from?"

A grim faced Brother Martin replied, "There is a simple explanation. All that Mr. Grubbs has comes from the blood of the poor people he has robbed."

From that day, the men at the monastery no longer asked Brother Martin to visit the lawyer.

Without Batting an Eye

This story of courage comes to us from the Orient.

When his advancing army stormed into a small town the general called his scouts before him. "Where are the citizens of this village?" he demanded.

"They have all fled in fear," the scouts replied.

"Is there no one left to pay tribute?" the general shouted.

"No one but the priest. He remains in the temple."

Quickly the general marched to the temple, burst through the doors and demanded to see the priest. After a search, the priest was found reading quietly in his study. The general, angry that the cleric refused to greet him as conqueror, shouted, "Don't you know that you are looking at one who can run you through without batting an eye?"

"Don't you know," the priest replied, "that you are looking at one who can be run through without batting an eye?"

For a moment the soldier stared in disbelief at the priest. Then, slowly, a smile danced on his lips. He bowed low and left the temple.

The Oak and the Ash

This fable from Aesop brings to mind the famous saying of the German pastor, Martin Niemoeller, "In Germany," he wrote, "they came first for the Communists, and I didn't speak up because I wasn't a Communist. Then they came for the Jews, and I didn't speak up because I wasn't a Jew. Then they came for the trade unionists, and I didn't speak up because I wasn't a trade unionist. Then they came for the Catholics, and I didn't speak up because I was a Protestant. Then they came for me, and by that time no one was left to speak."

A woodsman walked into a forest and asked the trees to provide him a handle for his axe. After a brief consultation, the trees offered the man a young ash tree. Immediately after he carved a new handle, the man began to cut down some of the noblest giants of the forest. An old oak, watching the destruction of his friends, spoke sadly, "We thought that providing the woodsman with our little brother, the ash, would satisfy him. Instead, our failure to protect the weak has contributed to our destruction."

Two Masters, One Load

A fable by Aesop.

"The enemy has duped the poor people," a man complained to the Teacher. "How can anyone be attracted to their ideology?"

"Let me tell you a fable," the Teacher said. "Once a shepherd spotted men from a hostile country approaching in the distance. 'Come quickly,' he said to his donkey, 'we must move with speed or we will be captured.'

'Pardon me,' the donkey replied slowly, 'but do you think the enemy will make me carry a larger load than you give me?'

'I don't suppose they will,' the man answered.

'Then as long as I have to carry heavy loads, what difference will it make to me whom I serve?' "

The Teacher looked at his angry friend, "Often the only difference a change in government makes to the poor is that they call their masters by different names."

Costly Advice

Most sources attribute this story to the great Indian leader, Mohandas Ghandi.

A mother approached the Teacher for assistance with a domestic matter. "My son has horrible eating habits," she said. "Please, he will listen to you if you tell him to stop eating foods with so much sugar."

The Teacher listened sympathetically. "I ask that you come back next week and make the request again."

The mother agreed and returned seven days later. "My son's problem continues," she said. "I am greatly concerned about his health. He rarely eats vegetables or fruits. Please, won't you talk to him about the danger of eating too much sugar."

"Please, come back and see me in a week," the Teacher said simply.

Though the mother was disappointed, she left and returned one week later. Once again she made her plea. This time the Teacher agreed to talk with her son.

When the conversation was completed, the mother thanked the Teacher. "I am grateful that you took the time to talk to my son, but I don't understand why it took three requests for you to do so."

The Teacher looked at the woman and said, "I didn't realize how hard it would be for me to give up sugar."

Night and Day

This story must have an impact for many people. Three different friends shared it with me.

The Teacher sat around a blazing fire with a small number of students late at night. Their meandering conversation was broken by periods of silence when they all gazed at the stars and the moon. Following one of these periods when no one spoke the Teacher asked a question. "How can we know when the night has ended and the day has begun?"

Eagerly one young man answered, "You know the night is over and the day has begun when you can look off in the distance and determine which animal is your dog and which is the sheep. Is that the right answer, Teacher?"

"It is a good answer," the Teacher said slowly, "but it is not the answer I would give," he said.

After several minutes of discussion a second student ventured a guess on behalf of the whole group, "You know the night is over and the day has begun when light falls on the leaves and you can tell whether it is a palm tree or a fig tree."

Once again the Teacher shook his head. "That was a fine answer, but it is not the answer I seek," he said gently.

Immediately the students began to argue with one another. Finally one of them begged the Teacher, "Answer your own question, Teacher, for we cannot think of another response."

The Teacher looked intently at the eager young faces before he began to speak. "When you look into the eyes of a human being and see a brother or sister you know that it is morning. If you cannot see a sister or brother you will know that it will always be night."

The Lion and the Boar

This peace story is adapted from a fable by Aesop.

One hot day in the middle of summer a lion and a boar went to a spring to drink. "Step aside," the boar said, "I was here first."

"I showed you where to find the spring," the lion replied angrily. "I will be the first to drink."

Quickly the disagreement escalated from a verbal confrontation and they began to attack each other with great ferocity. A few minutes later, stopping to catch their breath, they both saw some vultures seated on a rock above, waiting for one of them to be killed. The sight so sobered them that they quickly made peace saying, "If we continue to fight the only winner will be the vultures."

8

STORIES OF SIMPLICITY AND DISCIPLESHIP

Just a Pilgrim

A rich man stopped to visit the Teacher in his modest hut. He was astonished to see that such a famous man had but a wood table, some simple chairs, and a few books in his main room. "Teacher," the man asked, "where is your furniture?"

"I might ask the same question of you," the Teacher replied.

"I have no furniture because I am just a pilgrim. I am just passing through."

The Teacher smiled, "So am I."

Soap and Religion

This story is based on a Jewish tale.

As the Teacher was speaking with a group of children, a soap-maker attempted to embarrass him. "How can you claim that religion is good and valid when there is so much suffering and evil in the world? What good are all the books and sermons that your religion has produced?"

The Teacher motioned to a small child to move through the crowd. "This is Eric," the Teacher said. "He is three. He is also dirty. I ask you, what good is soap when Eric and hundreds of children like him are dirty. How can you pretend that soap is effective?"

"What a foolish argument," the soapmaker protested. "If soap is to be effective it must be used."

"Precisely," the Teacher answered. "If the teachings of our master are to be effective, they must be used."

The Pot of Gold

Every day, just outside a small village in India, an old man sat crosslegged stirring ordinary dirt mixed with water in an old pot. After hours of stirring he reached into the pot and pulled out a large gold nugget. Day after day people watched him sit, and waited for the moment when he would reach for the gold nugget. When he pulled it out, they would murmur with amazement.

One day a brazen young man approached the old man and asked, "Will you show me how you do your trick?"

"Certainly," the old man replied. "It isn't difficult. All I have here is an ordinary pot, a simple stick, dirt that you can find anywhere, and water from the town well. I pour the dirt and the water into the pot and begin to stir. After a while a lump of gold forms, and I reach in and remove it."

Immediately the young man found a pot, stick, some dirt, and a small bucket of water. He poured the dirt and the water into the pot and began to stir. He stirred all day long, stopping frequently to see if the gold had begun to form. He continued stirring the next day, clear into the evening. But no matter how long he stirred, no gold nuggets could be seen. Not even a small one.

Finally, he went back to the old man for further instructions. "Tell me, step by step, what you have been doing," the old man said politely. Quickly the young man recounted everything he had done. When he finished, the old master thought for a moment. "It seems I neglected to include one important detail," he said. "While you stir you must never think about the gold."

A Matter of Use

This Vietnamese folktale brings to mind the teaching of James regarding the tongue. "With it (the tongue) we bless the Lord and Father, and with it we curse men, who are made in the likeness of God. From the same mouth comes blessing and cursing" (James 3:9-10).

A woman called her cook aside early one morning and said, "Tonight, when my beloved visits, I want you to cook the food that has the most pleasant taste in the whole world."

The cook quickly went to the market where he made his purchase. That night, after serving many appetizers, he announced, "The main dish tonight is tongue of pig."

The woman was most surprised at the cook's choice and asked, "Why have you determined this to be the most pleasant taste in the world?"

"When people love each other," the cook replied, "their tongues say pleasant and loving things to each other. So is the tongue not the most pleasant thing in the whole world?"

"You are not only a fine cook," the woman said, "you are also a philosopher."

The next day the woman again approached the cook, "Last night my beloved and I found your choice most interesting. This evening we would like you to prepare the most unpleasant thing in the whole world."

Once again the cook made his way to the market to make a purchase. That evening he again served a variety of small dishes before announcing, "The main course this evening is tongue of pig." When both the woman and her beloved expressed surprise at the choice the cook explained, "When people hate each other their tongues say the most unpleasant things to each other. Is the tongue not the most unpleasant thing in the whole world?"

Sell All

This story is based on Mark 10:17-22.

A student approached the Teacher with a question. "When Jesus told the man to sell all that he had and give it to the poor, did he mean that we must get rid of everything?"

The Teacher answered with a story: "Once there was a man who listened to the Scripture. One day he heard Jesus quoted as saying to the rich man, 'Go! Sell all that you have, give to the poor, and you will have riches in heaven, and come follow me.'

"The man stiffened. This was a word to him for he, like the rich man, was seeking salvation. First, he sold his car. After he gave the money away, he again listened, and heard Jesus say, 'Sell all!'

"Next he sold his house. After he gave the money away he listened again, and heard Jesus say, 'Sell all!'

"All that he had left was his Bible, which he sold for a few dollars. When he gave the money away, he again listened. This time he heard nothing."

The student said, "Teacher, I don't understand this story. Why did the man hear nothing?"

The Teacher answered, "He heard nothing because he sold the

one thing that brought him the voice of God. We are not asked to rid ourselves of those things that draw us close to the heart of God. Jesus told the man to sell everything because his possessions were an idol. We must rid ourselves of whatever stands in the way of God. Now you must decide whether the things you own bring you close or separate you from God."

Your Coat as Well

Two thieves barged into the room of an old man and demanded, "Show us all of your valuables. You might as well cooperate, there is no way you can stop us."

"And I don't want to stop you," the old man said. "Here take what money I have and anything that you can use."

Quickly the men went through the small room, taking what few items of value they could find. Just before they left one of the thieves opened the old man's small closet and spotted a new shirt. He tore it off the hanger and threw it into his sack.

As the two men left the house the old man grabbed a box that lay on the floor and ran to the door. "I didn't realize that you were interested in clothing," he shouted. "Here, take the coat that I just purchased this afternoon. I am certain it will fit you."

One of the thieves turned toward the old man and demanded, "Just what is your game, old man? Why are you offering me this coat?"

"I try as best I can to live by the commands of Christ," the old man replied. "He told his followers not to resist those who are evil and that if someone takes your shirt to offer him your coat as well" (Matthew 5:39-40).

The two men listened with amazement to the simple words of the old man. Then, they carried all of the items they had stolen back into the house.

As they left, the first man whispered, "Pray for us, old man."

The second one just shook his head and said, "I didn't know there were any Christians left in this world."

Nobody Needs It

A rich stranger arrived at a monastery carrying a large bag of coins. "I would like you to distribute these among the brothers," he said to the priest.

"The brothers do not need it," the priest replied.

But the stranger was so persistent that the priest finally accepted the money, placed it in a basket at the entrance of the church and posted a handlettered sign over the basket that read: "Whoever needs it may take some."

After several days no one either touched the basket or even looked at it. The priest took the coins to the stranger and said, "God has accepted your offering. You gave these gifts out of a generous heart. Now, take your money and give it to the poor."

And he did.

The Peacock and the Crane

This story is based on a fable by Aesop.

A peacock fanned its gorgeous tail and then mocked the crane's plain plumage saying, "I am dressed like a king, wearing all the wonderful colors of the rainbow. You have not a bit of color on your wings." No sooner had the peacock finished his boasting than a hungry fox approached. As the crane soared over the terrified peacock he replied, "In moments like this I much prefer my plain, practical wings to your more elaborate ones."

9

STORIES OF CHRISTMAS AND OTHER FESTIVALS

The Story of St. Nicholas

On a day close to December 6, our church school commemorates the life of St. Nicholas. Children leave their shoes out in the hall where adults fill them with candy, toothbrushes, and small gifts. We also sing Christmas songs. Along with Christians throughout our country, we are attempting to deemphasize the secular aspects of the season by emphasizing our Christian roots. Our celebration is not complete without the telling of the story of the fourth century Christian bishop, Nicholas. Since information about the good bishop is sketchy and, as you will soon discover, highly legendary, the story is told lightly and with humor.

Nicholas was born around the year 280 in a small town in Asia Minor, which is present-day Turkey. His mother had long prayed for a child, and like Hannah in the Old Testament, had promised God that her firstborn would be dedicated to God's services. Even as an infant, Nicholas was a religious child. It is said that on holy days he would fast by refusing his mother's breast until after sunset.

Shortly after the turn of the century, Nicholas became Bishop of Myra where he was a kind and generous pastor. It was not an easy time to be a bishop, because the church faced enemies from both outside and within. When the emperor Diocletian began his ugly persecution of Christians, Nicholas and his people suffered. When Arius attempted to subvert the true teaching of the church, Nicholas helped gather a council at Nicaea in 325. He not only fought Arianism by helping to write the Nicene Creed that we still use today, but also boxed Arius alongside the head.

Perhaps the most famous story of Nicholas concerns a man who lived alone with his three lovely daughters. The poor man was not able to provide a dowry for any of his girls which meant that they would not be able to marry. Poor girls in those days either were sold into slavery or became prostitutes—both horrible choices. To save the eldest daughter, Nicholas placed a large number of gold pieces in a small bag and tossed it through an open window. Later he did the same for the two younger women. Though he attempted to provide the gifts anonymously, he was discovered by the father during his third visit. Many people think this is one of the origins of giving gifts at Christmas. During the middle ages, pictures of St. Nicholas always included three gold pouches.

St. Nicholas traditions developed in European countries under different names. In Germany he is Weihnachtsmann, Pere Noel in France, and Father Christmas in England. In Holland he is known either as St. Nicholas or Sinta Claes, from which we get Santa Claus.

The Dutch legend is said to have begun when Nicholas traveled to Holland from Myra, dressed in his red bishop's robes, riding a white horse, and accompanied by his servant Black Bart. As he rode the streets he carried a sack full of gifts for children—toys, oranges, and coins. Wherever he saw a child he asked their parents, "Has your child been good?" If the answer was yes the boy or girl received a gift. If the answer was no, Black Bart shook a stick at the children, who ran and hid behind their mother's skirts. People understood that the presents the good bishop delivered were gifts from God.

One day Nicholas and Black Bart came to a small hut where there were no windows and the doors were closed. "How shall we deliver our gifts?" Nicholas asked Bart.

Looking up at the roof, Black Bart suggested that they drop the presents through the chimney. "Splendid idea," the bishop exclaimed. The two men climbed the roof, dropped the gifts through the chimney. Miraculously, the gifts all landed in stockings that the children hung up to dry. Thus a new custom was born.

Few saints give inspiration to as many groups and nations as the gentle bishop of Myra. Even today he is claimed as the patron saint of students, sailors, travelers, and vagabonds. Through the legends he has shaped a noble tradition of generosity and kindness, particularly to children, during the season of our Savior's birth.

The Land of Fools

In this Chinese story, the second man enters the Land of Fools and shares the condition of the people much like Christ shared our human condition. In this way "The Land of Fools" becomes a story for Christmas.

Once a man strayed into the world known as the Land of Fools where he saw a number of people fleeing in terror from a field where they had been trying to harvest wheat. "There is a monster in that field," they told him. Upon close examination the man saw that it was a watermelon.

The stranger offered to kill the monster for them. He walked into the field, cut the melon from its stalk, took a slice and began to eat it. Now the people were more terrified of him than they had been of the melon. They drove him away with pitchforks crying, "He will kill us next, unless we get rid of him."

Years later a second man strayed into the Land of Fools and the same thing happened to him. But, instead of offering to help them with the monster, he agreed with them that it must be dangerous, and by tiptoeing away from it with them he gained their confidence. He spent a long time with them in their houses until he could teach them, little by little, the basic facts which would enable them not only to lose their fear of melons, but even to cultivate them.

The Rabbi's Gift

I have used this story by Francis Dorff at Christmas and Easter as well as many other occasions. This is truly a story for all seasons.

There was a famous monastery which had fallen on very hard times. Formerly its many buildings were filled with young monks and its big church resounded with the singing of the chant, but now it was deserted. People no longer came there to be nourished by prayer. A handful of old monks shuffled through the cloisters and praised their God with heavy hearts.

On the edge of the monastery woods, an old rabbi had built a little hut. He would come there from time to time to fast and pray. No one ever spoke with him, but whenever he appeared, the word would be passed from monk to monk: "The rabbi walks in the woods." And, for as long as he was there, the monks would feel sustained by his prayerful presence.

One day the abbot decided to visit the rabbi and to open his heart to him. So, after the morning Eucharist, he set out through the woods. As he approached the hut, the abbot saw the rabbi standing in the doorway, his arms outstretched in welcome. It was as though he had been waiting there for some time. The two embraced like long-lost brothers. Then they stepped back and just stood there, smiling at one another with smiles their faces could hardly contain.

After a while the rabbi motioned the abbot to enter. In the middle of the room was a wooden table with the Scriptures open on it. They sat there for a moment, in the presence of the Book. Then the rabbi began to cry. The abbot could not contain himself. He covered his face with his hands and began to cry too. For the first time in his life, he cried his heart out. The two men sat there like lost children, filling the hut with their sobs and wetting the wood of the table with their tears.

After the tears had ceased to flow and all was quiet again, the rabbi lifted his head. "You and your brothers are serving God with heavy hearts," he said. "You have come to ask a teaching of me. I will give you a teaching, but you can only repeat it once. After that, no one must ever say it aloud again."

The rabbi looked straight at the abbot and said, "The Messiah is among you."

For a while, all was silent. Then the rabbi said, "Now you must go."

The abbot left without a word and without ever looking back.

The next morning, the abbot called his monks together in the chapter room. He told them he had received a teaching from "the rabbi who walks in the woods" and that this teaching was never again to be spoken aloud. Then he looked at each of his brothers and said, "The rabbi said that one of us is the Messiah."

The monks were startled by this saying. "What could it mean?" they asked themselves. "Is brother John the Messiah? Or Father

Matthew? Or Brother Thomas? Am I the Messiah? What could this mean?"

They were all deeply puzzled by the rabbi's teaching. But no one ever mentioned it again.

As time went by, the monks began to treat one another with a very special reverence. There was a gentle, wholehearted, human quality about them now which was hard to describe but easy to notice. They lived with one another as men who had finally found something. But they prayed the Scriptures together as men who were always looking for something. Occasional visitors found themselves deeply moved by the life of these monks. Before long, people were coming from far and wide to be nourished by the prayer life of the monks and young men were asking, once again, to become part of the community.

In those days, the rabbi no longer walked in the woods. His hut had fallen into ruins. But, somehow or other, the old monks who had taken his teaching to heart still felt sustained by his prayerful presence.

The Other Wise Man

This well-known story by Henry Van Dyke is often used at Epiphany.

In ancient Persia lived a man named Artaban. He was a tall, dark man with brilliant eyes. His robe was pure white wool thrown over a tunic of white silk; and a pointed cap rested on his flowing black hair. It was the dress of the ancient priesthood of the Magi.

One December night, he told his friends, "My three friends are watching at the ancient temple in Babylon. If the promised star appears, they will wait 10 days for me, and then we will set out together for Jerusalem, to see and worship the One who shall be born King of Israel. I have sold my possessions, and bought these three jewels—a sapphire, a ruby, and a pearl—to carry them as tribute to the King."

While he was speaking he thrust his hand into the inmost fold of his girdle and drew out three great gems—one blue as a fragment of the night sky, one redder than a ray of sunrise, and one as pure as the peak of a snow mountain at twilight.

As Artaban watched the eastern sky that night, a steel-blue spark was born out of the darkness. It pulsated in the enormous vault as if the three jewels had mingled and been transformed into a living heart of light.

"It is the sign," he said. "The King is coming, and I will go to meet him."

At nightfall on the 10th day, Artaban was only three hours away from the temple where he was to meet his friends. Suddenly, his horse stood stock-still before a dark object in the road. The dim starlight revealed the form of a man lying there, moaning.

Artaban's heart leaped to his throat. How could he stay here to care for a dying stranger? What claim had this unknown fragment of human life upon his compassion or his service? The three Wise Men would go on without him. Should he risk the great reward of his faith for the sake of a single deed of charity?

"God of truth and purity," he prayed, "direct me in the holy path, the way of wisdom which thou only knowest."

Then he dismounted and carried the man to a little mound at the foot of a palm tree. Hour after hour he labored to comfort and help the stranger. At last, the man's strength returned.

To Artaban he whispered, "I have nothing to give thee in return—only this: I am a Jew, and our prophets have said that the Messiah for whom you seek will be born not in Jerusalem, but in Bethlehem. May the Lord bring thee in safety to that place, because thou hast had pity upon the sick."

It was now past midnight. The three Wise Men had gone on without Artaban across the desert. Artaban covered his head in despair. "I must sell my sapphire, and buy a train of camels, and provisions for the journey."

He arrived in Bethlehem three days after the three Wise Men had departed, after seeing the Christ child. He entered the open door of a cottage and found a young mother singing her baby to sleep.

In her gentle speech, she told him, "Joseph of Nazareth took the child Jesus and his mother Mary and fled away secretly in the night."

Suddenly, there came the noise of a wild confusion in the streets of the village and a cry: "The soldiers! The soldiers of Herod! They are killing our children."

The young mother's face grew white with terror, and she clasped her child to her bosom, and crouched in the darkest corner of the room.

Artaban went quickly and stood in the doorway. The soldiers came hurrying down the street with bloody hands and dripping swords.

The captain of the guard approached, and Artaban said in a low voice, "I am all alone in this place, and I am waiting to give this jewel to the prudent captain who will leave me in peace."

The captain stretched out his hand and took the ruby. "March on!" he cried to his men; "There is no child here."

Artaban turned to the east and prayed, "God of truth, forgive me. Two of my gifts are gone. Shall I ever be worthy to see the face of the King?"

The woman, weeping for joy, said: "Because thou hast saved the life of my little one, may the Lord bless and keep thee; the Lord make his face to shine upon thee and be gracious unto thee; the Lord lift up his countenance upon thee and give thee peace."

Artaban, the other Wise Man, traveled from country to country, searching for the King. In all this world of anguish, though he found none to worship, he found many to help. He fed the hungry, and clothed the naked, he healed the sick, and comforted the captive.

Three-and-thirty years had passed. Worn and weary and ready to die, but still looking for the King, he came for the last time to Jerusalem. Excitement was flashing through the city's crowds.

"Have you not heard what has happened?" they asked Artaban. "Today they are crucifying Jesus of Nazareth, who says he is the Son of God and the King of the Jews."

Artaban's heart beat unsteadily. "I have come in time to offer my pearl in ransom for the King's life," he thought.

A group of soldiers came down the street dragging a girl. She broke suddenly from her tormentors and threw herself at Artaban's feet.

"Save me," she cried. "I am to be sold as a slave. Save me!"

Was this his great opportunity or his last temptation? Twice, the gift he had for God had gone to serve man.

He took the pearl from his bosom. Never had it seemed so luminous, so radiant. He laid it in the hand of the girl. "This is thy ransom. It is the last of my treasures which I kept for the king."

While he spoke, a shuddering earthquake rocked the city, and the sky grew dark. A heavy tile fell and struck the old man on the temple. The girl bent over him. She heard a voice come through the twilight, like music from a distance. The girl turned to see if someone had spoken from the window above them, but she saw no one.

Then the old man's lips began to move, as if in answer: "Not so, my lord: For when did I see thee hungry and feed thee? Or thirsty and give thee drink? When did I see thee a stranger, and take thee in? Or naked, and clothe thee? When did I see thee sick or in prison, and come unto thee? Three-and-thirty years have I looked for thee; but I have never seen thy face, nor ministered to thee, my King."

He ceased, and the sweet voice came again. And again the

maid heard it, very faintly and far away. But now it seemed as though she understood the words:

"Verily I say unto thee, Inasmuch as thou hast done it unto one of the least of these my brethren, thou hast done it unto me."

A calm radiance of joy lighted the pale face of Artaban like the first ray of dawn on a snowy mountain-peak. One long, last breath of relief exhaled gently from his lips.

His journey was ended. His treasures were accepted. Artaban had found the King.

The Tinker King

I have told this tale, adapted from a story by James Carroll, for the festival of Christ the King, the Sunday before Advent.

There was once a king who disliked the ceremony and trappings of his office. He reluctantly wore a crown and was uncomfortable when forced to sit on the throne. It began the day of his coronation when they brought him a magnificent ermine robe. "Where did this robe come from?" asked the young king.

The courtier replied, "It came from the royal merchant."

"Where did this robe come from?" the king repeated.

"Why, it came from Persia," the baffled courtier replied.

"Where did this robe come from?" the king persisted.

Finally the courtier blurted, "Majesty, this robe comes from the skins of small animals whom the hunters trap!"

Sadly, the king touched the robe and said, "How can I wear such cruelty for a robe?"

Another time a prince brought a pearl of immense value to the king as a gift. "Receive this pearl as a sign of my homage," he said to the king.

"Why is this pearl so valuable?" the king asked.

"Because of its perfect, moonlike shape," replied the prince.

But the king persisted asking his question until the flustered prince confessed, "This pearl is valuable because sixteen male slaves drowned while trying to retrieve it from the ocean floor."

Sadly, the king refused the gift saying, "How can I wear such cruelty for a jewel?"

Though he disliked all the trappings of his office, he replaced them only with confusion. He canceled the Christmas feast when he discovered that the food was taken as a tax from the peasants, but he could not think of another way to celebrate. He took no steps to change the customs of the kingdom, but was only saddened by them. People said he was too sensitive and gentle to be a king, and he agreed. One day, he simply walked away from the palace and never returned.

Quickly a cohort of cruel knights replaced the gentle king. They increased the taxes and reveled in the splendor of royalty. As taxes rose, services deteriorated. Roads and bridges were no longer repaired and sanitary conditions grew worse.

Meanwhile, the gentle king became a tinker and traveled about the country sharpening knives and fixing pots. Most of his work was done in the kitchens of the peasants. They loved the little man who listened with his eyes and asked questions with his heart. The tinker and the people learned from each other.

He learned that the people were unhappy. He learned that the taxes of the knights created a terrible burden and that their inept rule made life difficult.

The people learned from the tinker that everything is connected to everything else and that whenever anything dies a little we all die a lot.

What the people did not learn from the tinker was the nature of his true identity. Although he looked like the former king, no one was certain. Why would a king be working as a tinker? Often people asked him, "Are you a king?" He normally responded by asking them a question, "Do I look like a king?"

One day the tinker was sharpening kitchen knives under a tree at the home of a family whose son had died in the fields while working long hours, trying to earn the monthly tribute tax. When a crowd gathered to talk, the tinker asked the father a question, "Who did this to your son?"

"The heat did it; the heat killed my son," the man replied sadly.

The tinker pressed him until the man cried out, "The knights did this. The cruel knights killed my boy!"

People quickly quieted the father telling him that such talk was dangerous. "The truth is always dangerous," the tinker said gently.

"What are we to do?" the boy's father pleaded. But the tinker did not reply. "You see connections," he cried. "You make us see connections with your questions. Now that we see, what are we to do?"

Looking up from the knife he was sharpening on his wheel, the tinker said quietly, "The knights have not always ruled this kingdom. One day they will be removed."

"How can we fight men with great swords," a woman in the crowd cried, "when all we have are farming tools?"

The tinker stood and faced the crowd. He spoke with a voice that was powerful and clear, "When the time comes, you will not use swords. All that will be needed will be stout poles. Begin now to collect them."

"Before we collect our poles," a voice shouted, "answer one question. Are you the king?"

This time the tinker did not even respond with another question. He simply waved his hand for the people to disperse, and they left.

A few days later the tinker stopped by the side of the road near the royal palace to work on his cart. Hearing hoof beats, he looked up to see a knight riding a giant stallion directly at him. He pulled up and stopped.

"What are you doing, you old fool?" the knight bellowed.

"I don't believe we have met," the tinker replied.

"I am one of the ruling knights," the man on horseback shouted, giving the tinker a kick that sent him rolling in the dirt. Then, spying the whet wheel on the cart he asked, "Are you a tinker?"

"I am," the old man said picking himself up.

"Then you are coming with me," the knight said triumphantly.

He tied a rope around the tinker and nearly dragged him into the royal courtyard. The knight dismounted and then yelled for all to hear. "Brothers, noble knights. I have brought a tinker to sharpen our weapons. Bring your swords and axes and the tinker will put fine edges on all our steel."

For three long days the tinker sat hunched over his wheel sharpening the weapons of the cruel rulers. Every blade in the palace was placed against his wheel. When he finished, the swords were so sharp that they could cut fine paper. The big knight pushed the tinker out through the city gates and jeered, "We have spared your life so that you can sharpen our weapons another day."

Quickly the tinker moved across the plain and up to a nearby village. He called the people together with a shout. No longer did he speak in questions. This time he gave directions. "The time has come. Gather at dawn tomorrow on the plain outside the palace. Bring your stout poles."

Before the sun rose all the people of the kingdom assembled near the castle where the cruel knights lived. Each carried a stout pole or a farming tool. In front of them, standing on his old cart, was the tinker.

When the great wooden doors of the castle wall opened the crowd of mounted knights appeared. Their swords and armor glistened in the morning light. As they began to move, fear seized the crowd.

"Stand tall, my people," cried the tinker.

"But we are about to die!" they shouted.

"No," the tinker insisted, "you are about to live. Do not strike these men, these cruel knights. They are your poorest sons. Only stop their swords with your sticks."

No one understood what the tinker meant, but trusting him, they stood firm, their poles held high above their heads. The knights roared with laughter at the sight of the peasants facing them with mere wood. The first knight went straight for the tinker and swung his sword as if to cut through the branch and kill him. As his sword slashed into the thin wood, instantly, remarkably, the metal withered and collapsed. The tinker in sharpening the knights' weapons to such fine edges had ground away their substance on his wheel. The swords were sharp to the eye and soft to the touch, but when they met the wood, they withered like tissue.

One by one the knights were disarmed. Without a single death, without a single injury, the battle was over.

All the people gathered around the old cart and cheered the tinker. One of the older citizens spoke for them all, "Once and for all answer the question we have all asked, are you a king?"

The tinker stepped forward and said with a voice that was strong and clear, "I am."

Immediately the crowd broke forth shouting, "Crown the tinker, crown the tinker!"

Holding up his hands for quiet, the old man addressed his supporters, "I am not a king who will rule over you. I have come not to be served, but to serve. I have come to help you see that everything is connected to everything else. I urge you to choose leaders who love justice and who live humbly and simply. Remember, the greatest among you must be a servant of all." And then he simply slipped away and let them begin a new life without him.

In the years ahead the little kingdom established a government that was just and fair. When people told stories to their children about the early days they said that their way of life had been shaped by the man who was called "the Tinker King."

Christmas in the Trenches

Frequently at Christmas we get so caught up with love and sentiment that we forget that the coming of the Christ child caused deep tremors in the social landscape. He was not just a cute little baby, but the one "who put down the mighty from their thrones and exalted those of low degree." For centuries people have confessed that once they meet the incarnated Son of God, nothing is ever the same.

On Christmas Eve in 1914, the first year of World War I, a strange quiet had settled on the western front. It was a welcome respite for a group of lonely English soldiers who had become all too familiar with the roar of the cannons and the whine of the rifles.

As they reclined in their trenches each man began to speculate about the activities of loved ones back home. "My parents are just finishing a toast to my health," a lad from Liverpool said slowly.

"I can almost hear the church bells," a stout man from Ely said wistfully. "My whole family will soon be walking out the door to hear the concert of the boy's choir at the cathedral."

The men sat silent for several minutes before a thin soldier from Kent looked up with tears in his eyes. "This is eerie," he stammered, "but I can almost hear the choir singing."

"So can I," shouted another puzzled voice. "I think there is music coming from the other side."

All the men scrambled to the edge of the trench and cocked their ears. What they heard was a few sturdy German voices singing Martin Luther's Christmas song, "From heav'n above to earth I come, to bear good news to every one. Glad tidings of great joy I bring to all the world, and gladly sing."

When the hymn was finished, the English soldiers sat frozen in silence. Then a large man with a powerful voice broke into the chorus of "God rest ye merry gentlemen." Before he had sung three bars a dozen voices joined with him. By the time he finished the entire regiment was singing.

Once again there was an interlude of silence until a German tenor began to sing "Stille Nacht." This time the song was sung in two languages, a chorus of nearly a hundred voices echoing back and forth between the trenches, "Silent night, holy night! All is calm, all is bright. . . ."

"Someone is approaching!" a sentry shouted, and attention was focused on a single German soldier who walked slowly, waving a white cloth with one hand and holding several bars of chocolate in the other. Slowly, men from both sides eased out into the neutral zone and began to greet one another. In the next golden moments each soldier shared what he had with the others, candy, cigarettes and even a bit of Christmas brandy. Most important the soldiers showed the battered, but treasured pictures they carried of loved ones.

No one knows whose idea it was to start the football match, but with the help of flares the field was lit and the British and German soldiers played until they and the lights were exhausted. Then, as quietly as they came together, the men returned to their own trenches.

On Christmas day, men from both sides again joined together, even visiting the other's trenches. The German soldiers, wishing to avenge the previous night's torch-lit football loss, organized another game of what Americans call soccer.

In a few days the cannons once again boomed across "no man's land" and the whine of rifles was again heard in the trenches. For some, however, it was never the same. The enemy was no longer faceless. Now he was an acquaintance who shared a candy bar or played soccer. When men looked down the barrels of their guns at the opposition they also saw the smiling faces of those whose pictures were shared on a silent, holy night when the birth of the Christ child drew hostile forces together as brothers and, for a few moments, gave weary soldiers a taste of peace and good will.

NOTES

1. Larry Rasmussen, "Shalom: The Ancient Vision Ahead" (unpublished paper), p. 1.
2. Walter Wink, *Transforming Bible Study* (Nashville: Abingdon, 1980), p. 32.
3. C. S. Lewis, *Surprised by Joy* (New York: Harcourt, Brace, and Co., 1955), p. 63.
4. Ibid., p. 60.
5. Ibid., p. 115.
6. Walter Hooper, *Past Watchful Dragons: The Narnian Chronicles of C. S. Lewis* (New York: Collier Books, 1971), p. 20.
7. Lewis, *Surprised by Joy*, p. 170.
8. Ibid.
9. Shelia Daily, "The Hidden Country in C. S. Lewis's *Chronicles of Narnia*" (unpublished Master's thesis, Central Michigan University, 1982), p. 9.
10. Ibid., p. 10.
11. Lewis, *Surprised by Joy*, p. 226.
12. Ibid., p. 223-224.
13. Ibid., p. 237.
14. Wink, op. cit., p. 32.
15. Andrew M. Greeley, *The Religious Imagination* (New York: Sadlier, 1981), p. 87.
16. Dailey, op. cit., p. 10.
17. C. S. Lewis, *Of Other Worlds: Essays and Stories,* ed. Walter Hooper (New York: Harcourt and Brace, 1966), p. 29-30.

BIBLIOGRAPHY

Aesop's Fables. Based on a translation by George Fyler Townsend. Garden City: Doubleday, 1968 (Out of print; other editions available).

Ausubel, Nathan, ed. *A Treasury of Jewish Folklore: Stories, Traditions, Legends, Humor, Wisdom and Folk Songs of the Jewish People*. New York: Crown, 1948.

Bash, Ewald. *Visit to Five Brothers and Other Double Exposures*. St. Louis: Concordia, 1968.

Bausch, William J. *Storytelling: Imagination and Faith*. Mystic, Connecticut: Twenty-Third Publications, 1984.

The World Over Story Book: An Illustrated Anthology for Jewish Youth. Ed. Belth Norton. New York: Bloch Publishing Company, 1952.
Belth's collection includes a few folktales and wisdom stories along with a large number of short stories by Jewish authors and brief biographic tales of famous Jewish people.

Brown, Raphael. *The Little Flowers of St. Francis*. Garden City: Doubleday and Company, 1958.

Bryant, Sara Cone. *The Burning of the Rice Fields*. New York: Holt, Rinehart, and Winston, 1963.
A delightful Japanese tale comes alive in this illustrated story.

Calvino, Italo. *Italian Folktales*. New York: Harcourt, Brace, Jovanovich, 1980.

This book of 200 stories by a gifted writer includes a number of mythological stories about the days when Jesus and Peter walked the earth long after the resurrection.

Chekov, Anton. *The Image of Chekov: Forty Stories by Anton Chekov in Order in Which They Were Written.* Trans. Robert Payne. New York: Knopf, 1971.

This is one of several sources of Anton Chekov's story, "The Student."

Dailey, Shelia. "The Hidden Country in C. S. Lewis's *Chronicles of Narnia.*" (Unpublished Master's thesis, Central Michigan University, 1982).

This paper is the best piece I have found on the subject of Lewis's use and understanding of imagination.

Downing, Charles. *Tales of the Hodja.* New York: Henry Z. Walck, Inc., 1965.

Downing retells the stories of Nasreddin (his spelling).

Eisenberg, Aziel, ed. *Tzedakah: A Way of Life.* New York: Behrman House, 1963.

Eisenberg has collected nearly 30 Jewish stories of charity and self-giving.

Evans, Lawton B. *Old Time Tales.* Springfield: Milton Bradley, 1922.

Among the many treasures in this collection is the story of "Jerome and the Lion."

Fritz, Jean. *The Man Who Loved Books.* New York: Putnam, 1981.

Fritz tells the story of Columba, the beloved Irish saint.

Greeley, Andrew M. *The Religious Imagination.* New York: William H. Sadler, Inc., 1981.

This sociological study by Greeley and his associates points to faith-shaping experiences of Catholic young adults. He concludes that story has a great power in the development of the religious imagination.

Green, Roger Lancelyn, and Walter Hooper. *C. S. Lewis: A Biography.* New York: Harcourt, Brace, Jovanovich, 1974.

Hodges, Margaret. *The Wave.* Boston: Houghton Mifflin, 1963.

This is another version of the Japanese folktale that I have called "The Burning of the Rice Fields."

Hooper, Walter. *Past Watchful Dragons: The Narnian Chronicles of C. S. Lewis.* New York: Collier Books, 1971.

Kaye, Danny. *Danny Kaye's Around the World Story Book.* New York: Random House, 1960.

Levin, Meyer. *Classic Hassidic Tales.* New York: Dorset Press, 1931.

Lewis, C. S. *Of Other Worlds: Essays and Stories.* Ed. Walter Hooper. New York: Harcourt, Brace, Jovanovich, 1966.

Lewis, C. S. *On Stories: And Other Essays on Literature.* Ed. Walter Hooper. New York: Harcourt, Brace, Jovanovich, 1966.

Lewis, C. S. *Surprised by Joy: The Shape of My Early Years.* New York: Harcourt, Brace, and Co., 1955.

> Like most of Lewis's books, his spiritual autobiography is written with humility, insight, and wit.

Linney, Romulus. *Jesus Tales.* San Francisco: North Point Press, 1980.

> This book is based on mythical stories of Jesus that are found in Italian folklore. At times the stories are amusing; at times they are absurd. At all times they are enjoyable reading.

Lohfink, Gerhard. *Jesus and Community: The Social Dimension of Christian Faith.* Trans. John P. Galvin. Philadelphia: Fortress Press, 1984.

McCormick, Carol, ed. *In the Way of Peace: Stories of Vision and Action.* Plymouth, Minnesota: The Story Peddlers, 1985.

> McCormick has compiled nearly 20 peace stories as a result of her involvement in the Minnesota Peace Child Project.

McNamara, William. *Earthy Mysticism.* New York: Crossroads, 1983.

> The author, a trappist monk, includes a chapter on prayer and storytelling.

Nahmad, H. M. *A Portion in Paradise and Other Jewish Folktales.* New York: The Viking Press, 1970.

> This book includes tales of the Prophet Elijah and King David and King Solomon.

Newland, Mary Reed. *The Saint Book.* New York: The Seabury Press, 1979.

> The author paints brief portraits of more than 55 saints arranged by the date of their feast days.

Nouwen, Henri. *The Way of the Heart.* New York: Ballantine Books, 1981.

Nouwen's book on solitude, silence, and prayer draws heavily on the writings of the Desert Fathers.

Rapaport, Samuel. *A Treasury of the Midrash.* New York: KTAV Publishing House, 1968.

The title is an apt description of the contents of the book.

Rasmussen, Larry. "Shalom: The Ancient Vision Ahead." (Unpublished paper.)

Shah, Idries. *The Caravan of Dreams.* London: Octagon, 1968.

The author is the foremost collector of Sufi stories and other tales from the Islamic tradition.

Tolstoy, Leo. *The Short Stories of Leo Tolstoy.* New York: Bantam, 1960 (Out of print).

Most of these stories come from Tolstoy's later years when he was writing on religious subjects. Many of his stories are adapted from other writers or from folktales.

Tresmontant, Claude. *A Study of Hebrew Thought.* New York: Desclee Company, 1960.

Tresmontant compares Hebrew and Greek thinking.

Ward, Benedicta. *The Sayings of the Desert Fathers.* London: Mowbrays, 1975.

The "sayings" include a large number of teaching stories from that early Christian monastic movement.

Wharton, Fr. Paul. *Stories and Parables for Preachers and Teachers.* New York: Paulist Press, 1986.

Fr. Wharton has collected about 100 stories and has provided several helpful indexes.

White, William. *Speaking in Stories: Resources for Christian Storytellers.* Minneapolis: Augsburg, 1982.

This book is an introduction to the art of storytelling, answering the important how and why questions. It contains nearly 40 stories.

White, William. *Stories for Telling: A Treasury for Christian Storytellers.* Minneapolis: Augsburg, 1986.

This is a collection of 60 stories with essays on storytelling in ministry and the power of TV.

Wiesel, Elie. *The Gates of the Forest.* New York: Holt, Rinehart, and Winston, 1966.

Wiesel, Elie. *Messengers of God: Biblical Portraits and Legends.* New York: Random House, 1976.

Drawing on the Midrash of the Jewish scriptures, Wiesel paints portraits of Adam, Cain, Jacob, Moses, and other Old Testament figures.

Wink, Walter. *Transforming Bible Study.* Nashville: Abingdon, 1980.

This book includes an essay on the meaning of the two hemisphere theory of the brain and its implications for Bible study.